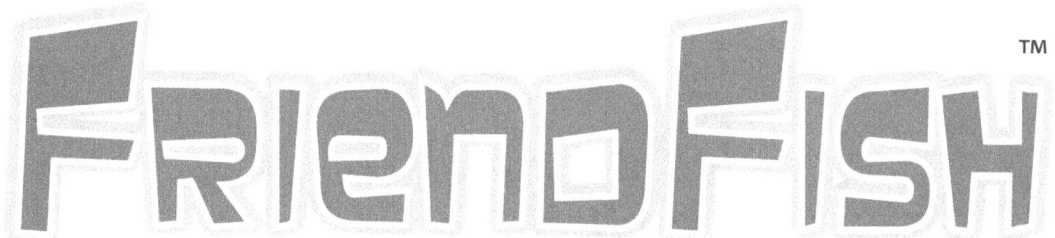

CREATED BY JOHN-MARC GROB

I0432281

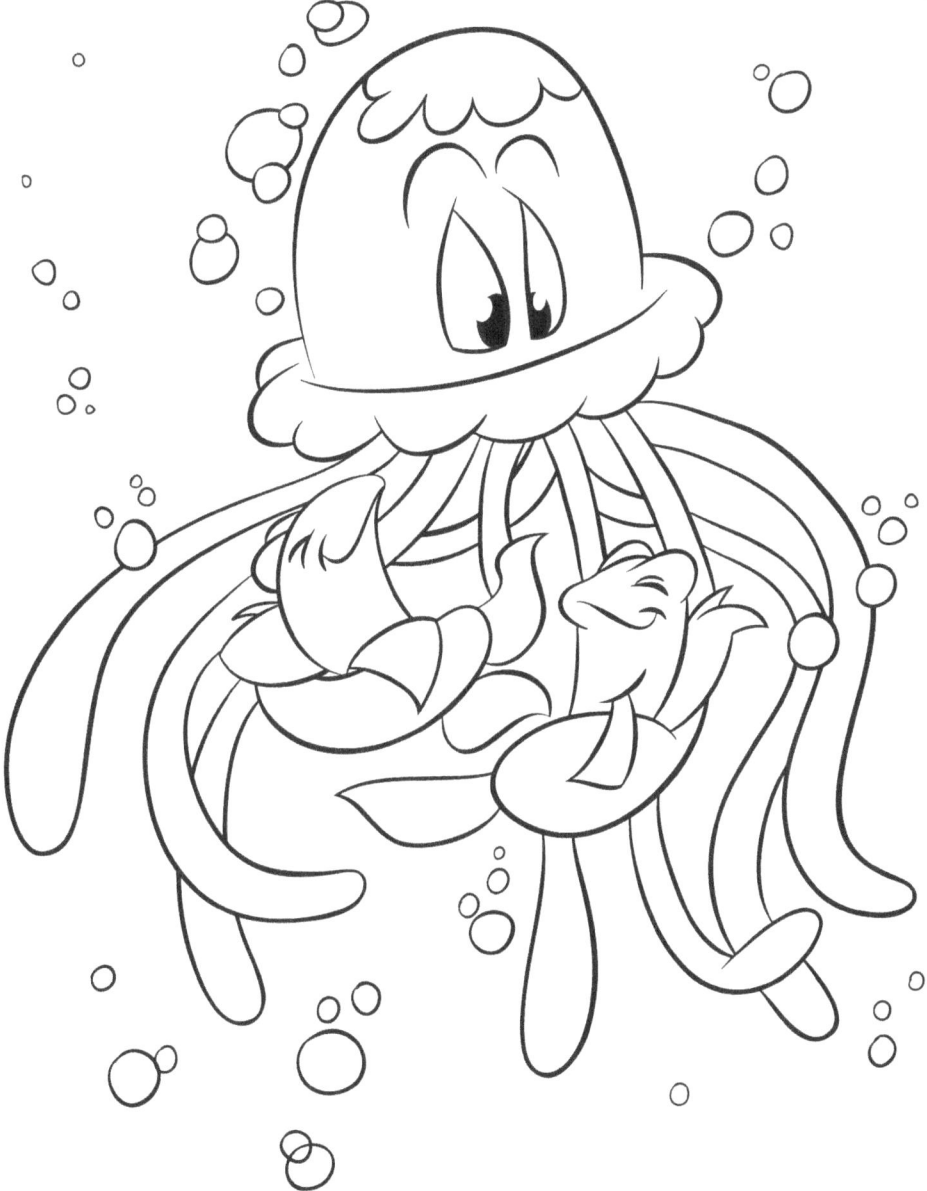

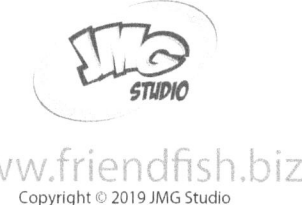

www.friendfish.biz
Copyright © 2019 JMG Studio

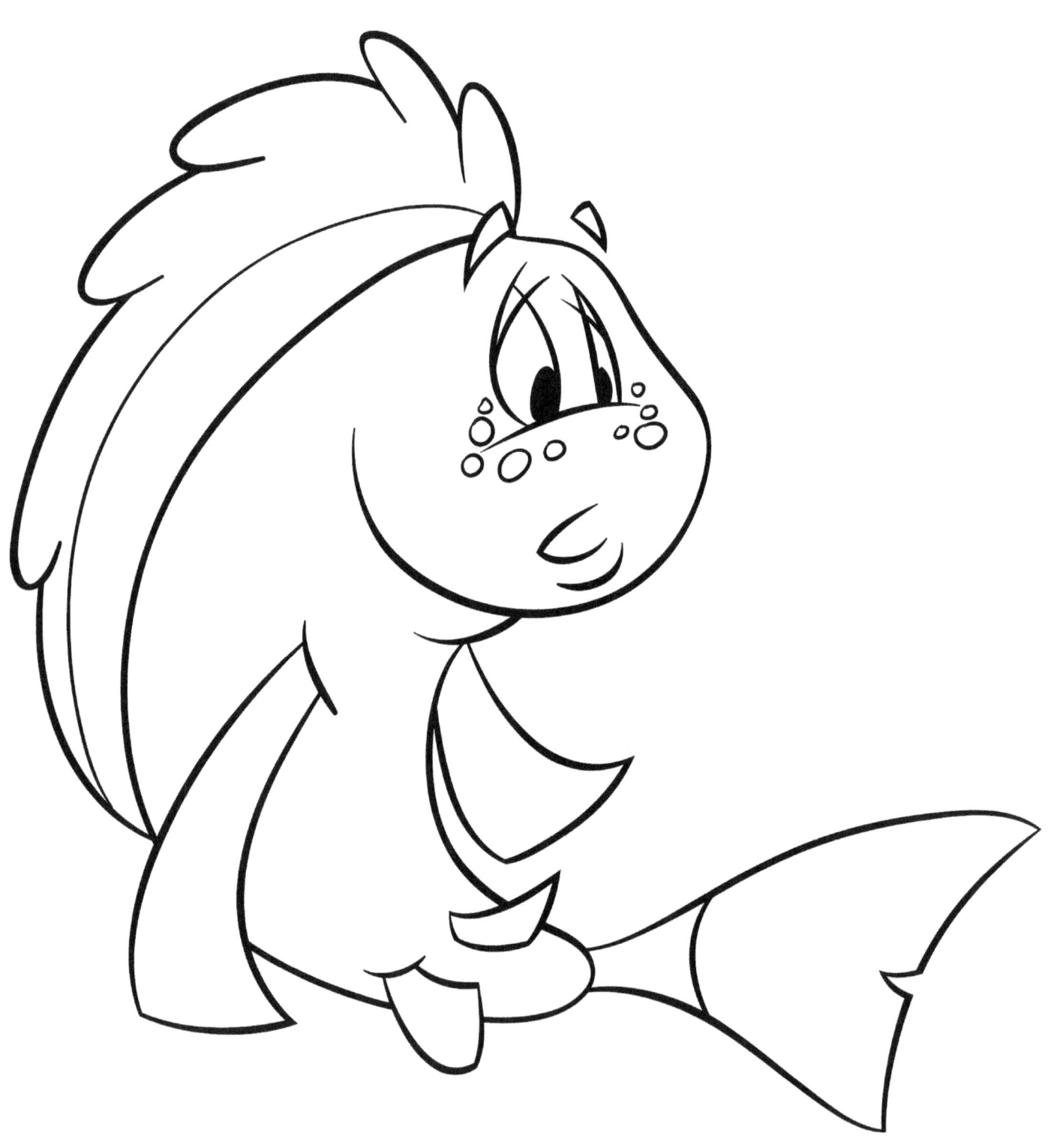

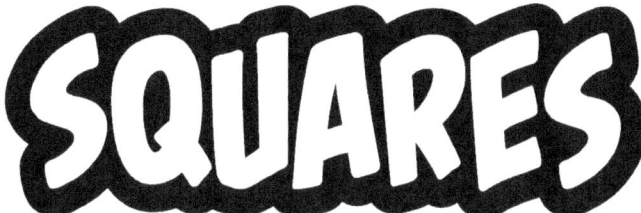 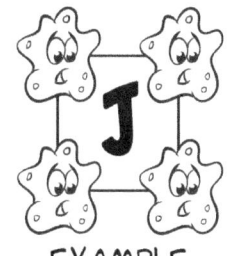

EXAMPLE

TAKE TURNS, CONNECT A LINE FROM ONE PLANKTON TO ANOTHER. WHOEVER MAKES THE LINE THAT COMPLETES THE BOX PUTS THEIR INITALS INSID THAT BOX. THE PERSON WITH THE MOST SQUARES AT THE END OF THE GAME WINS!

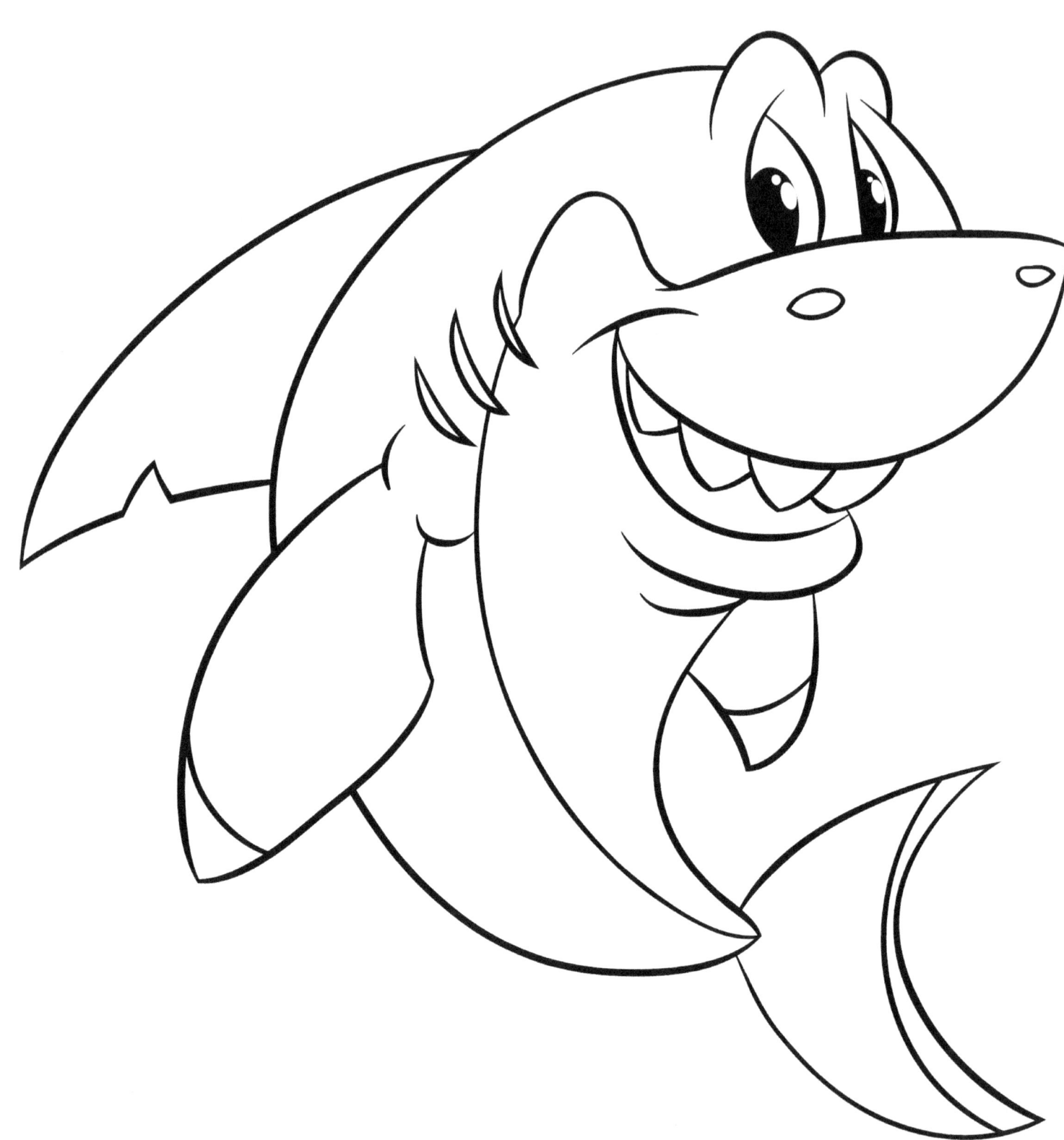

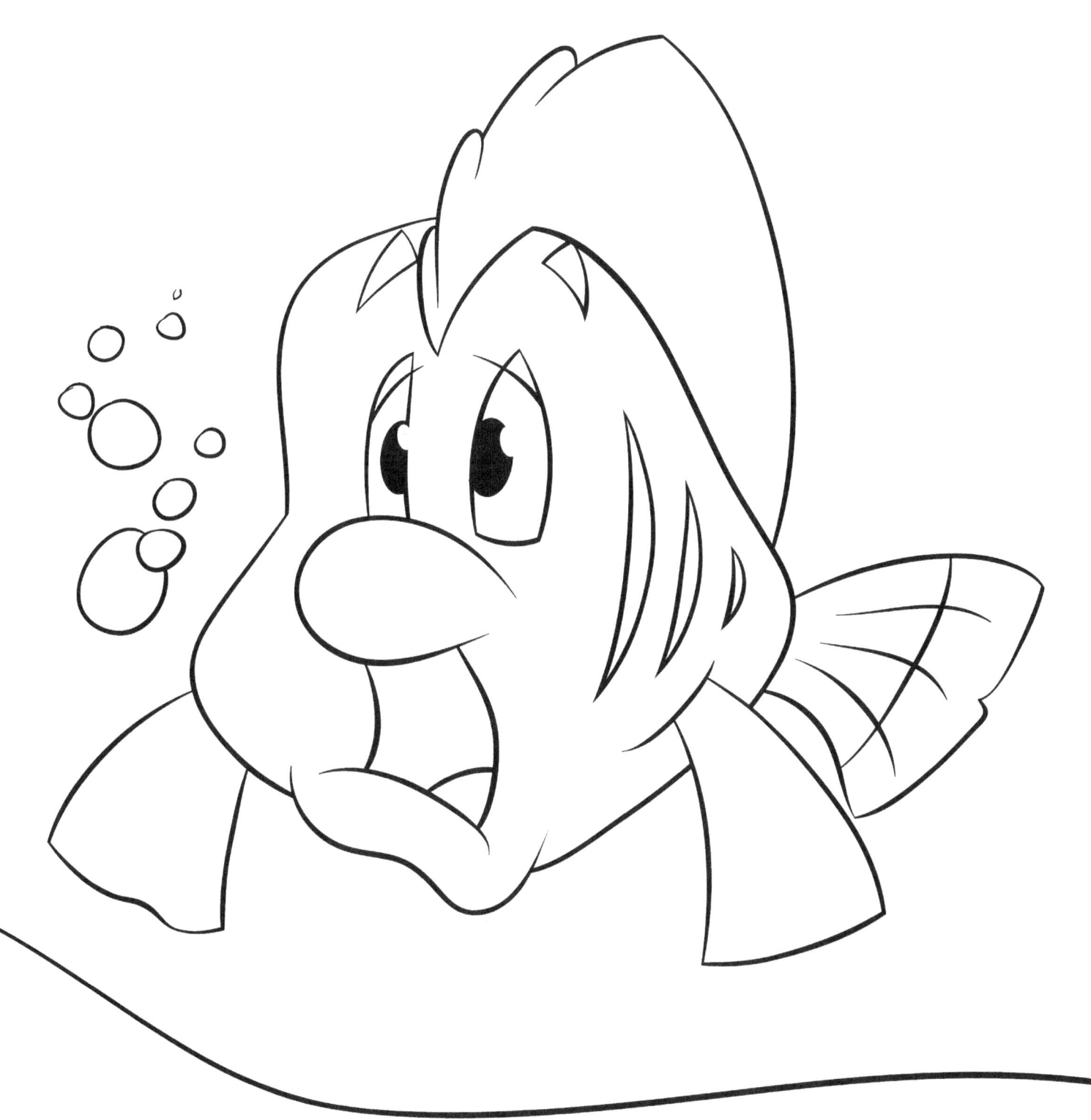

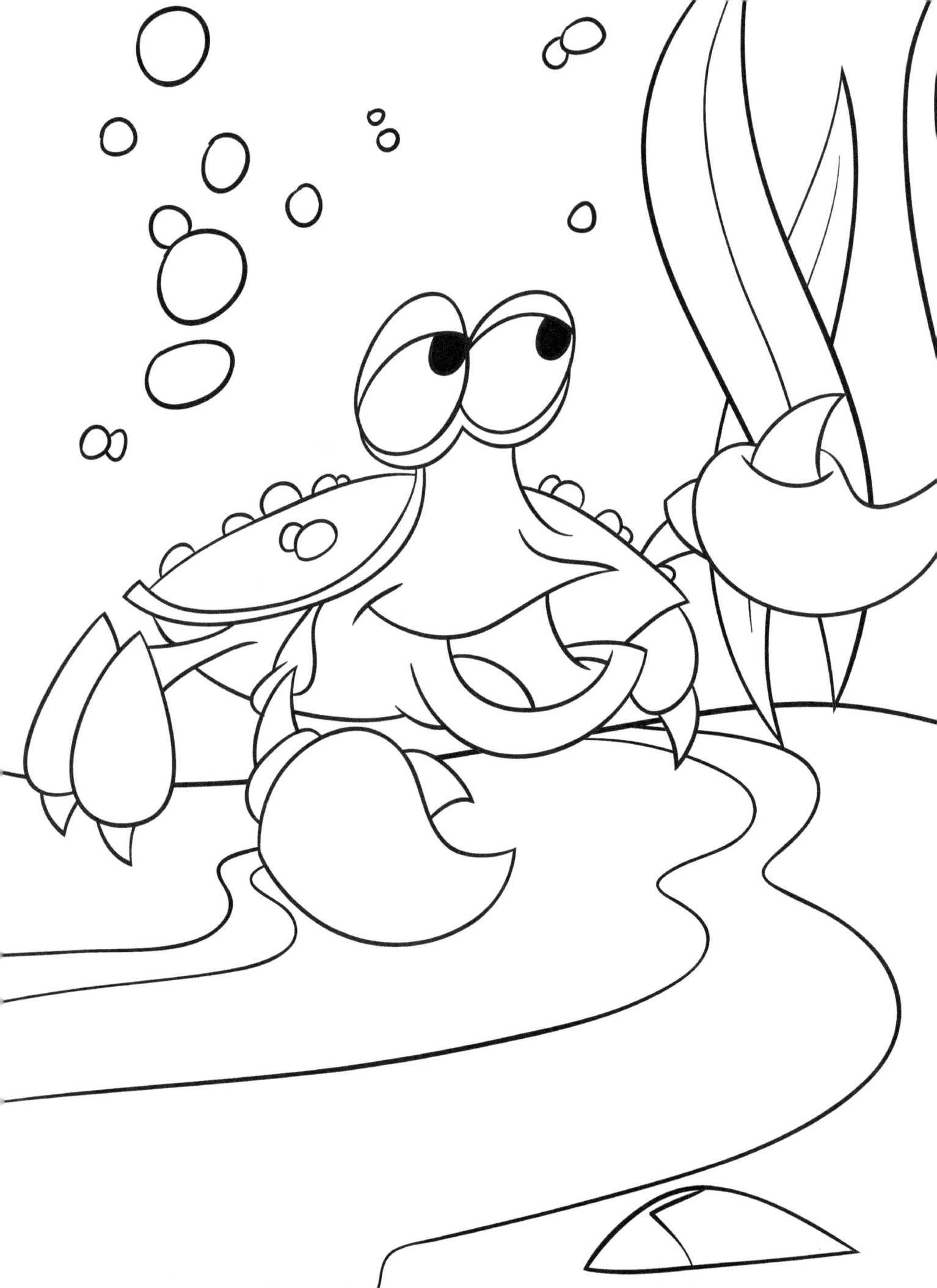

Find the Different Picture

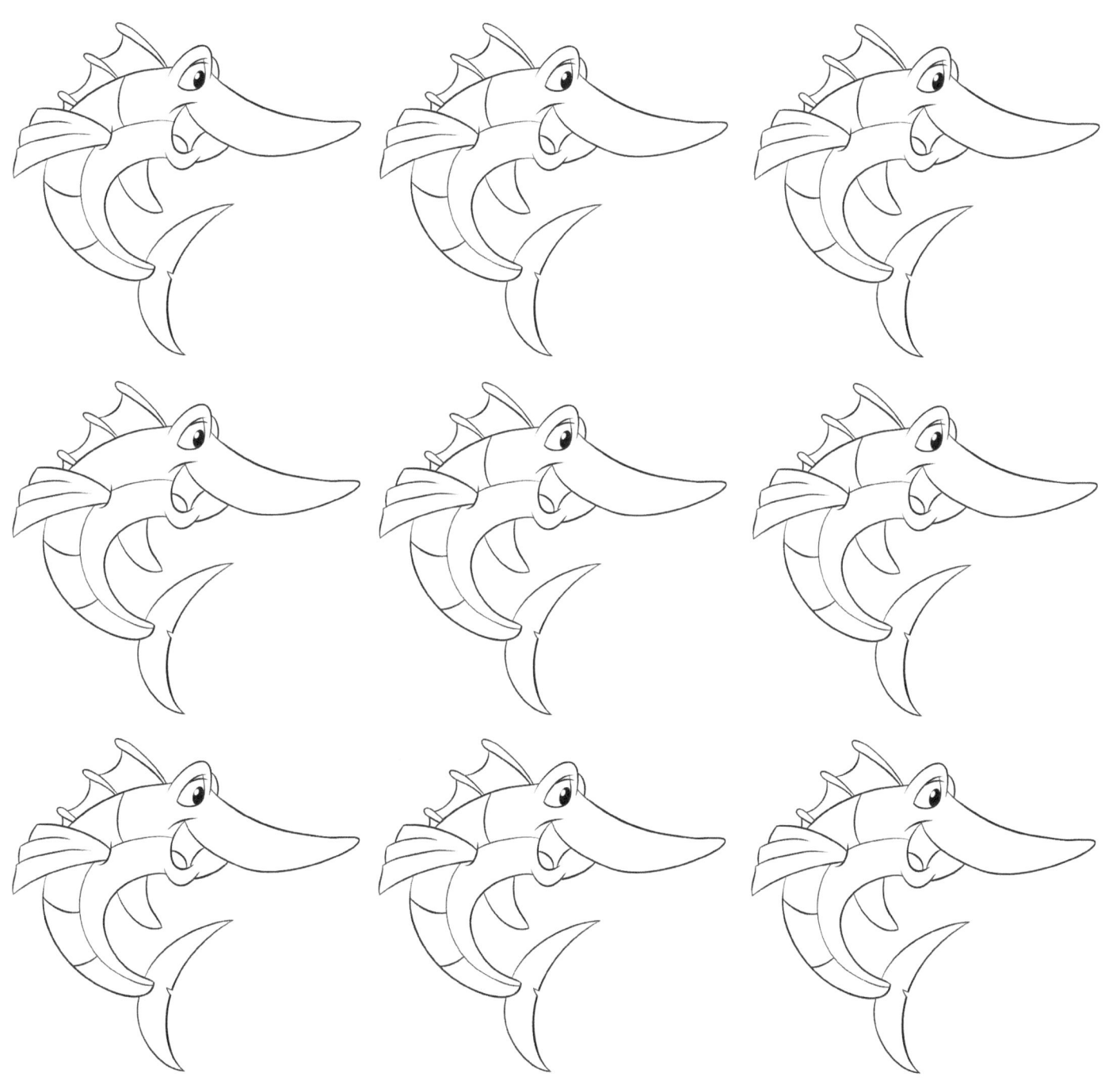

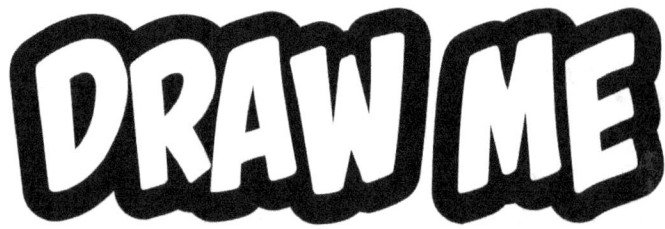

USE THE GRID TO HELP
YOU DRAW THIS FISH.

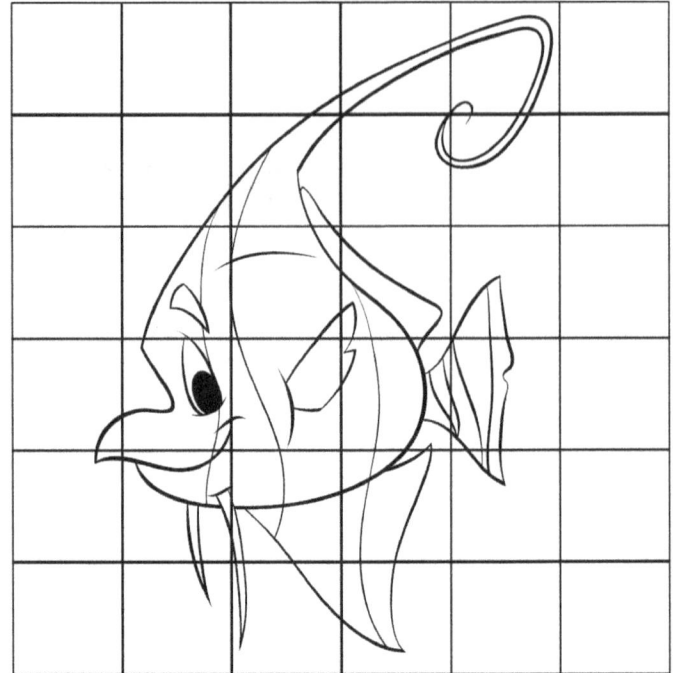

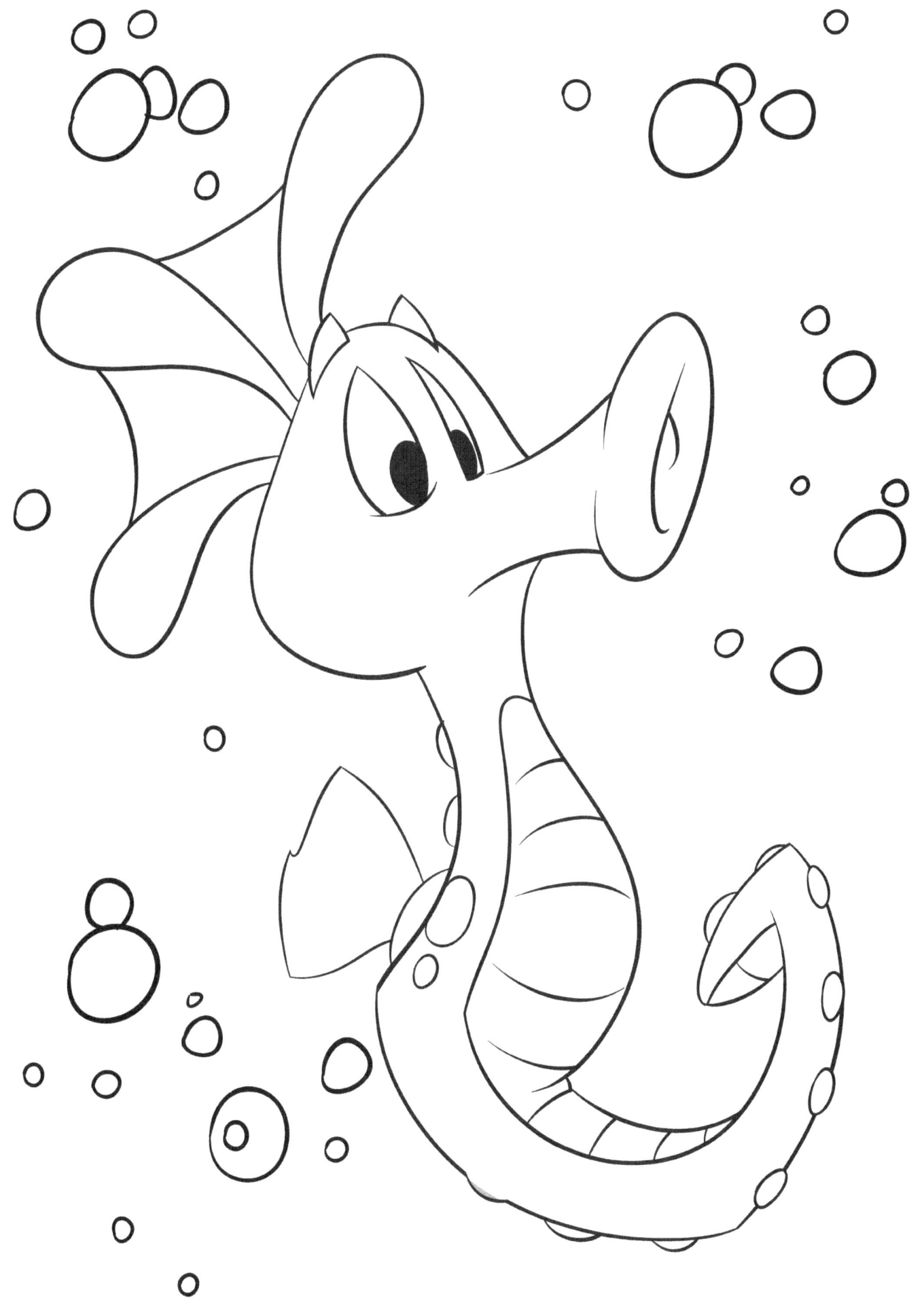

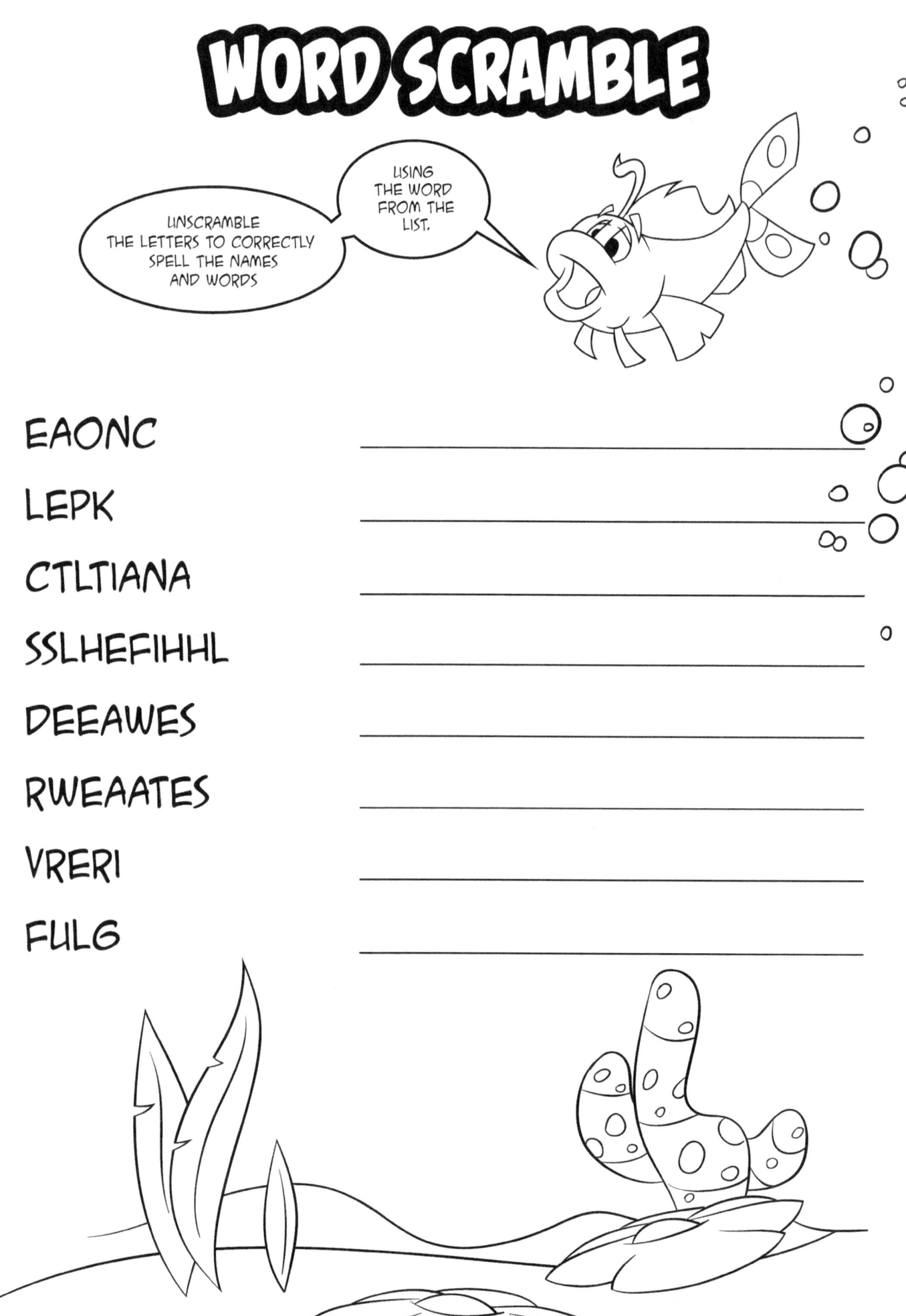

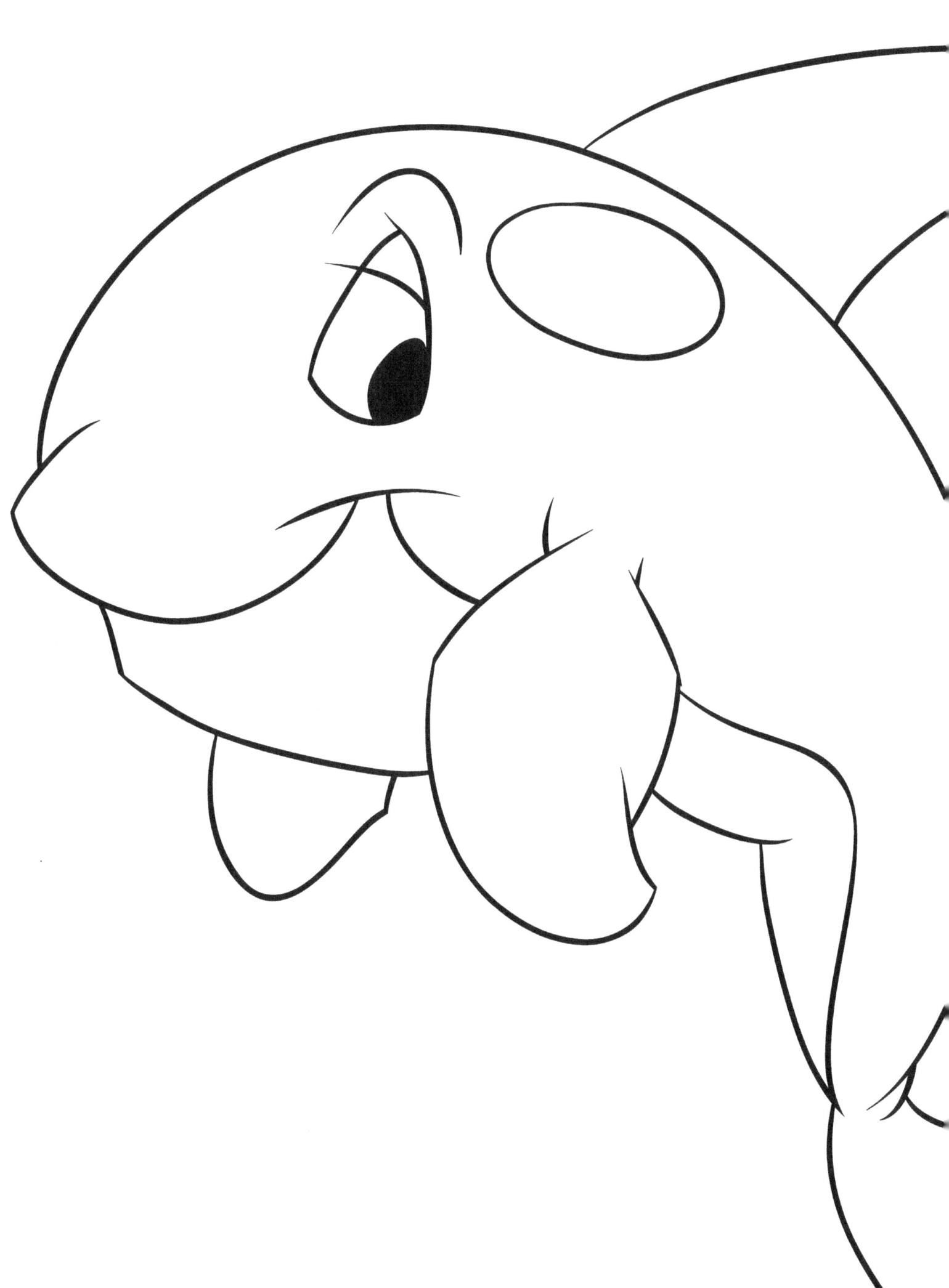

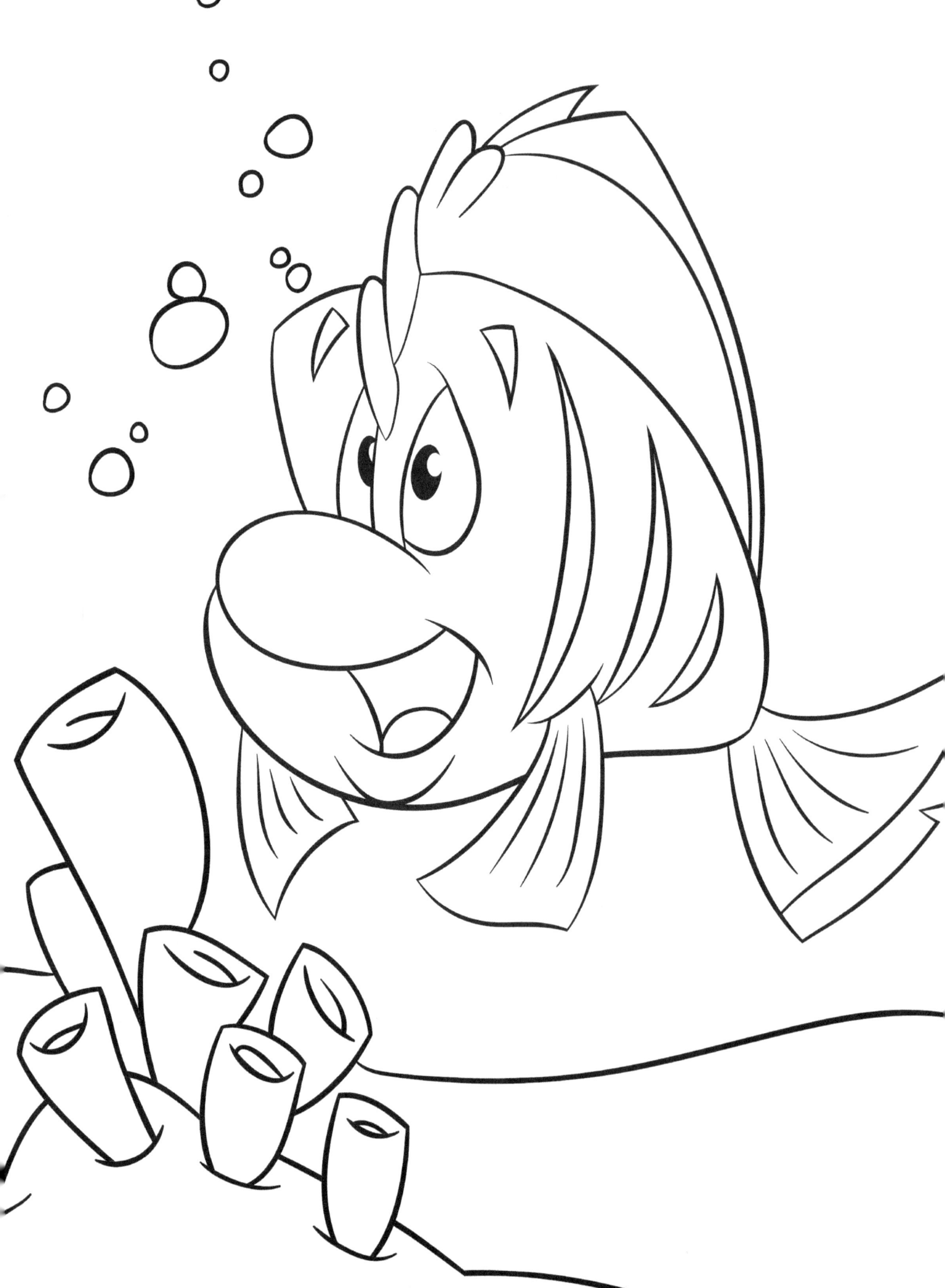

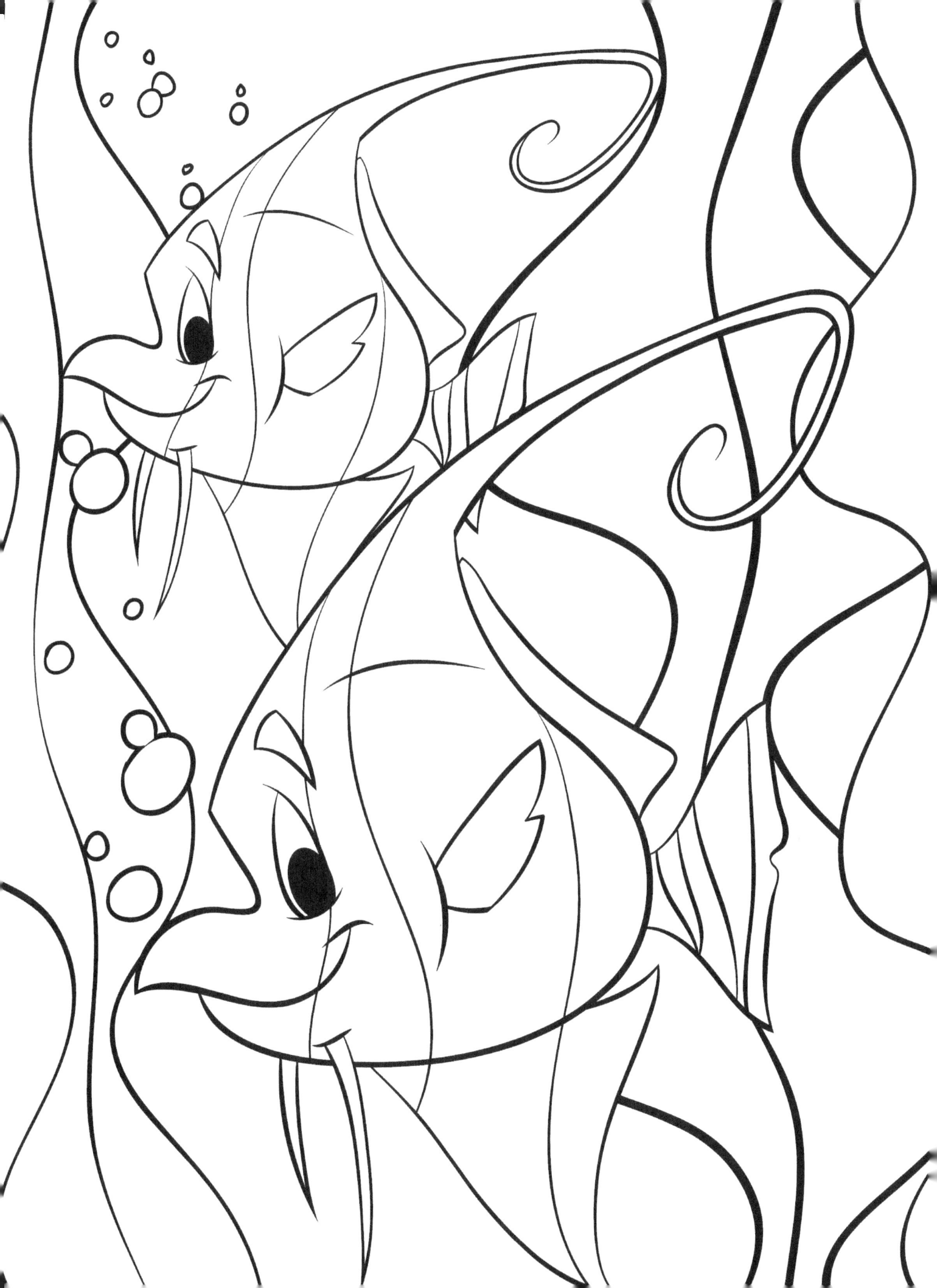

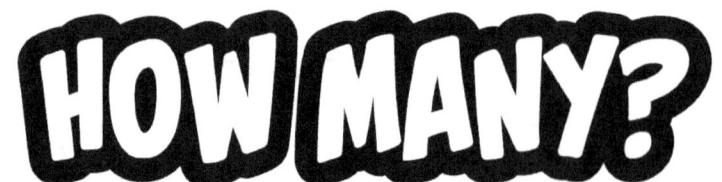

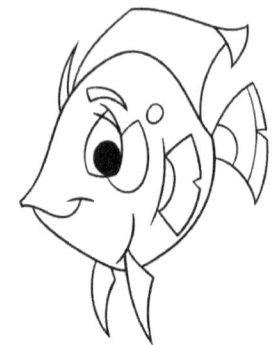

HOW MANY WORDS CAN YOU MAKE USING THE LETTERS BELOW.

HUMPBACK WHALE

EXAMPLE: PEA

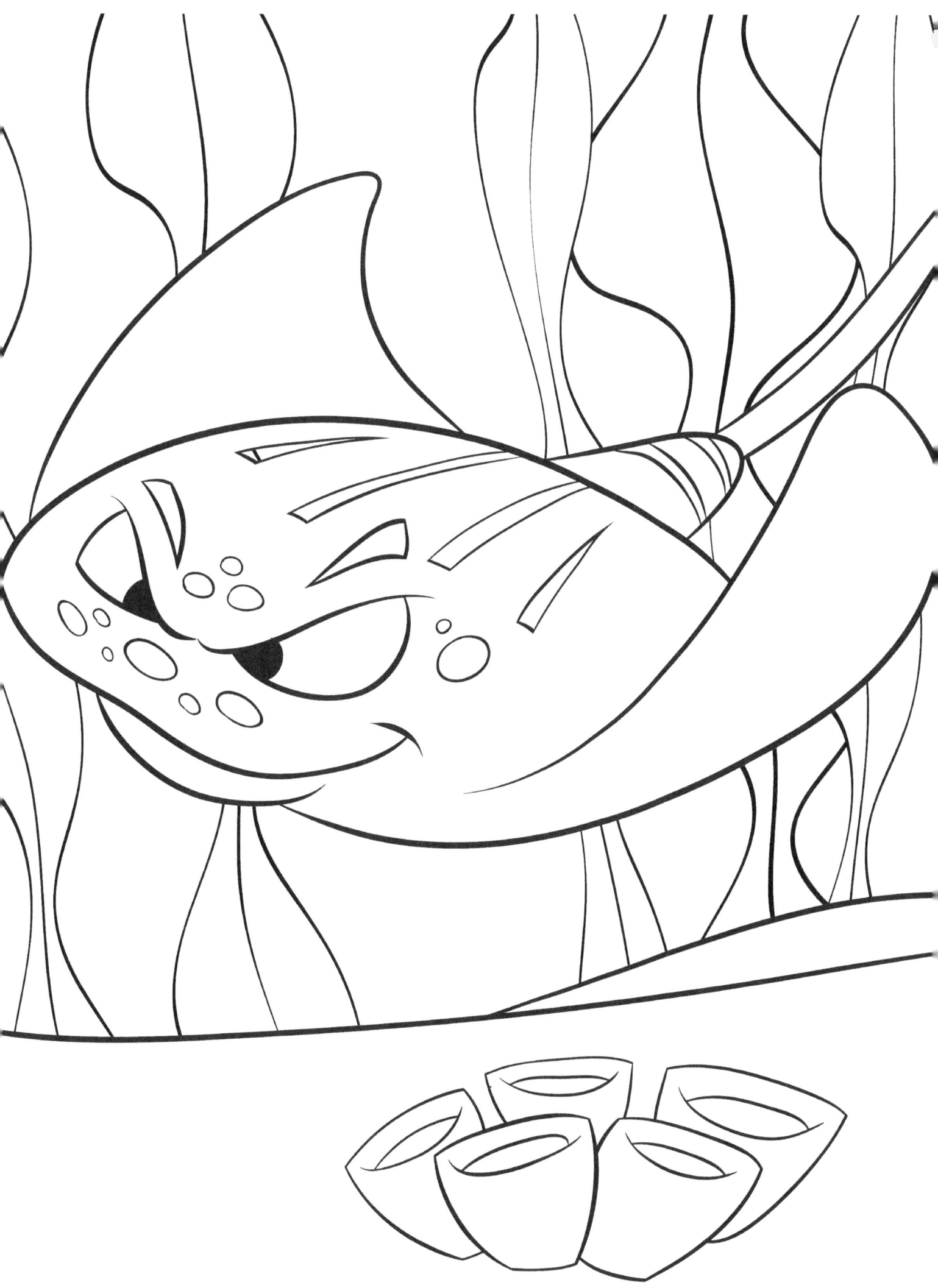

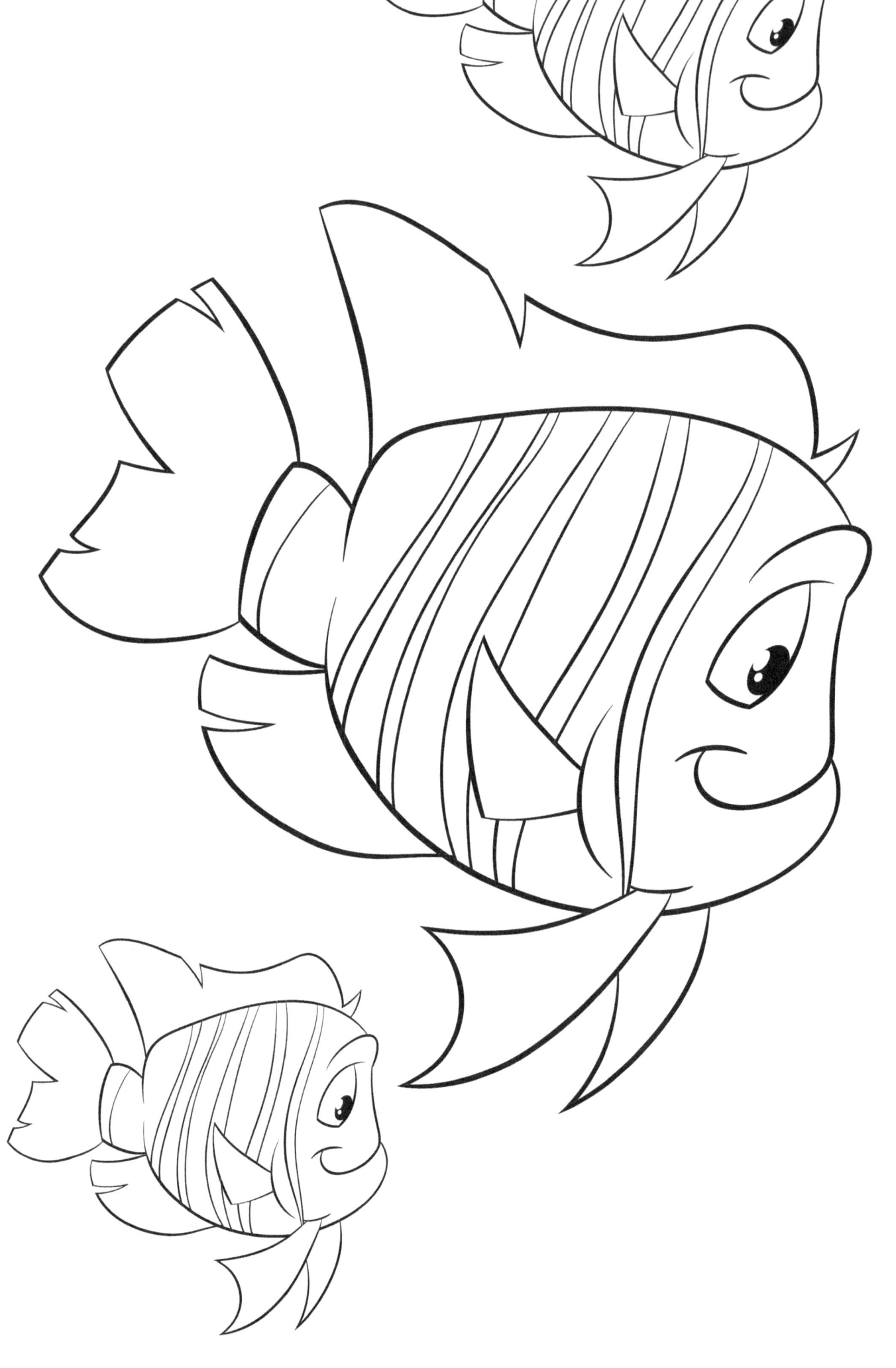

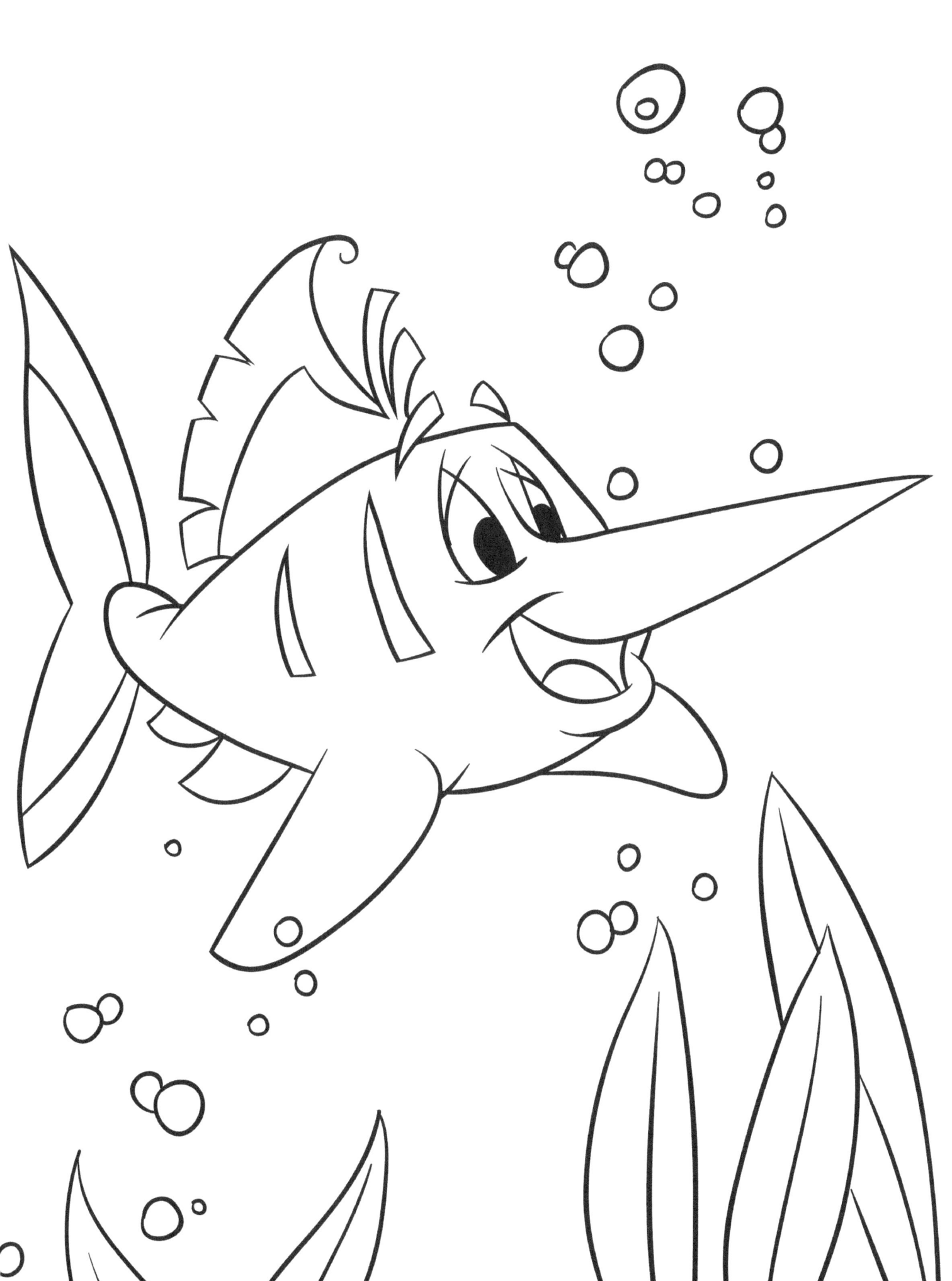

TIC-TAC-TOE

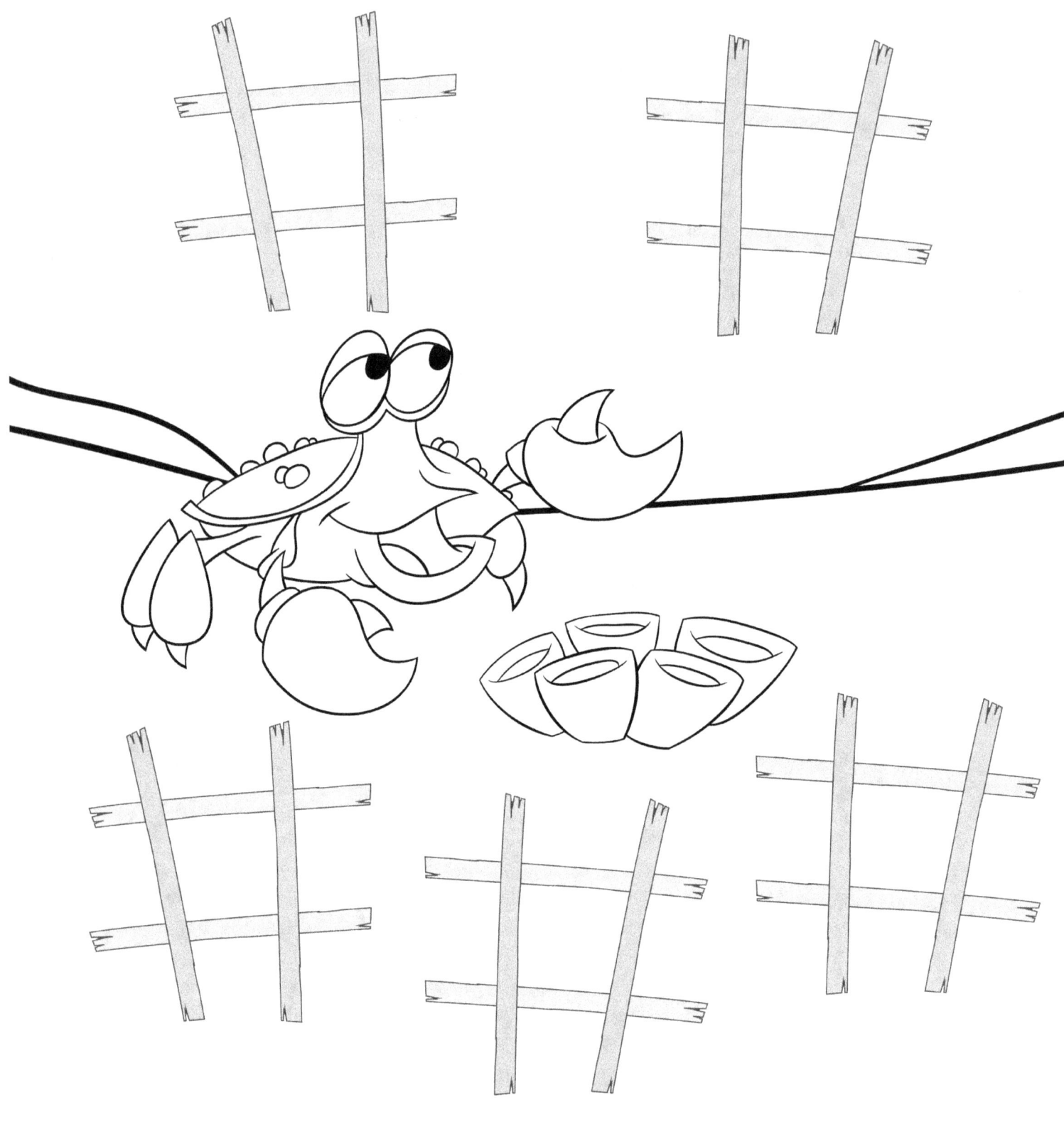

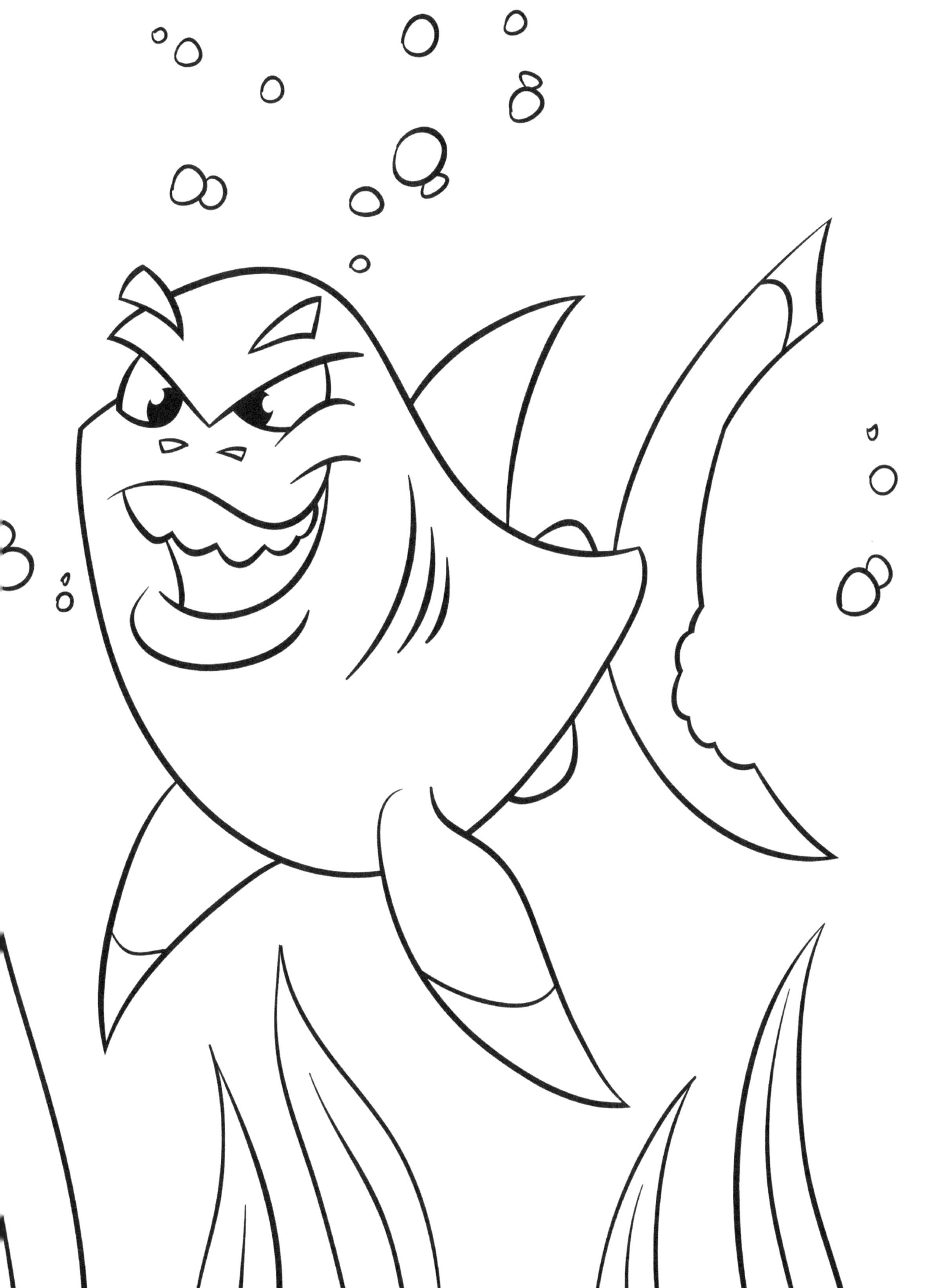

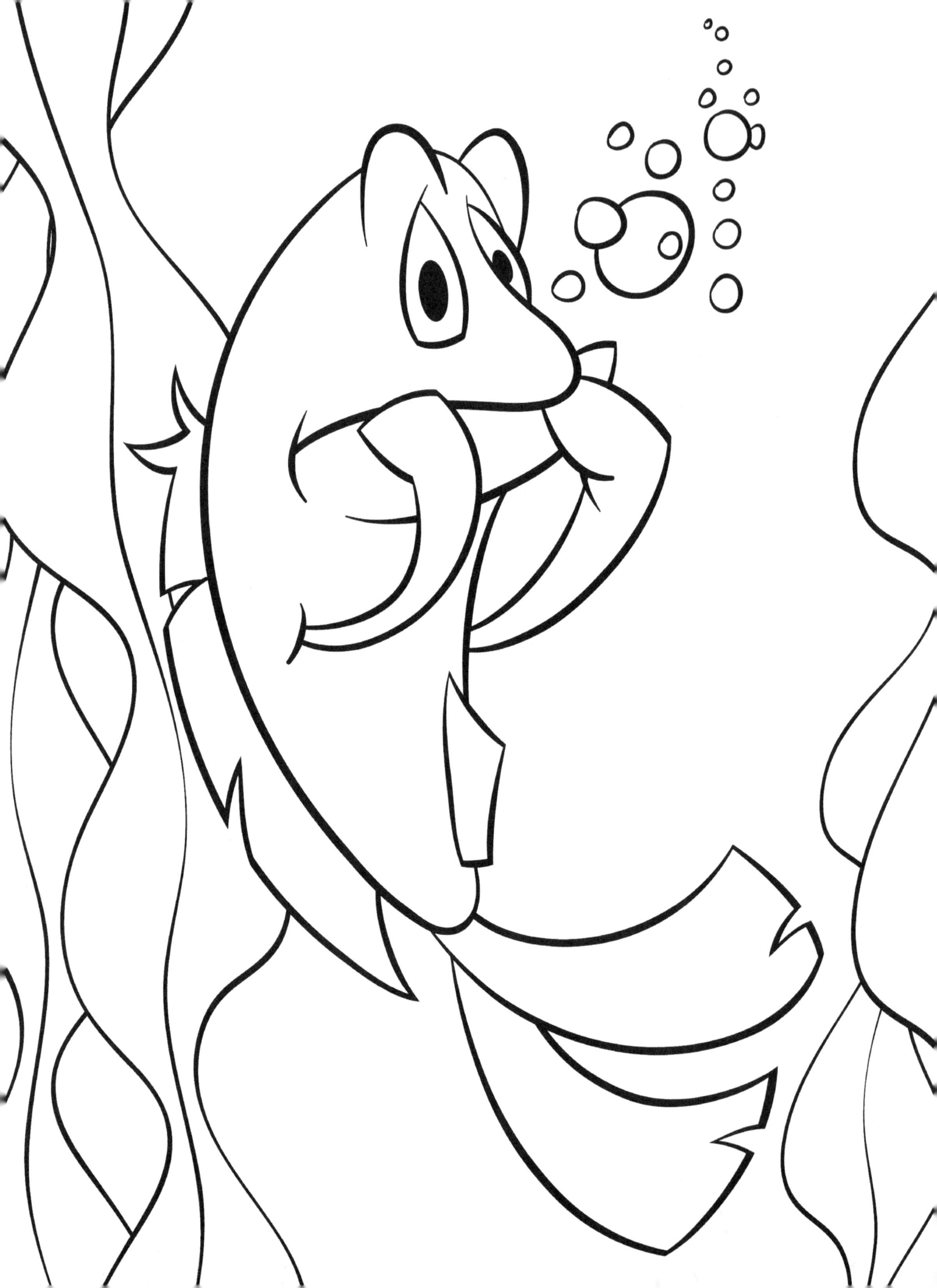

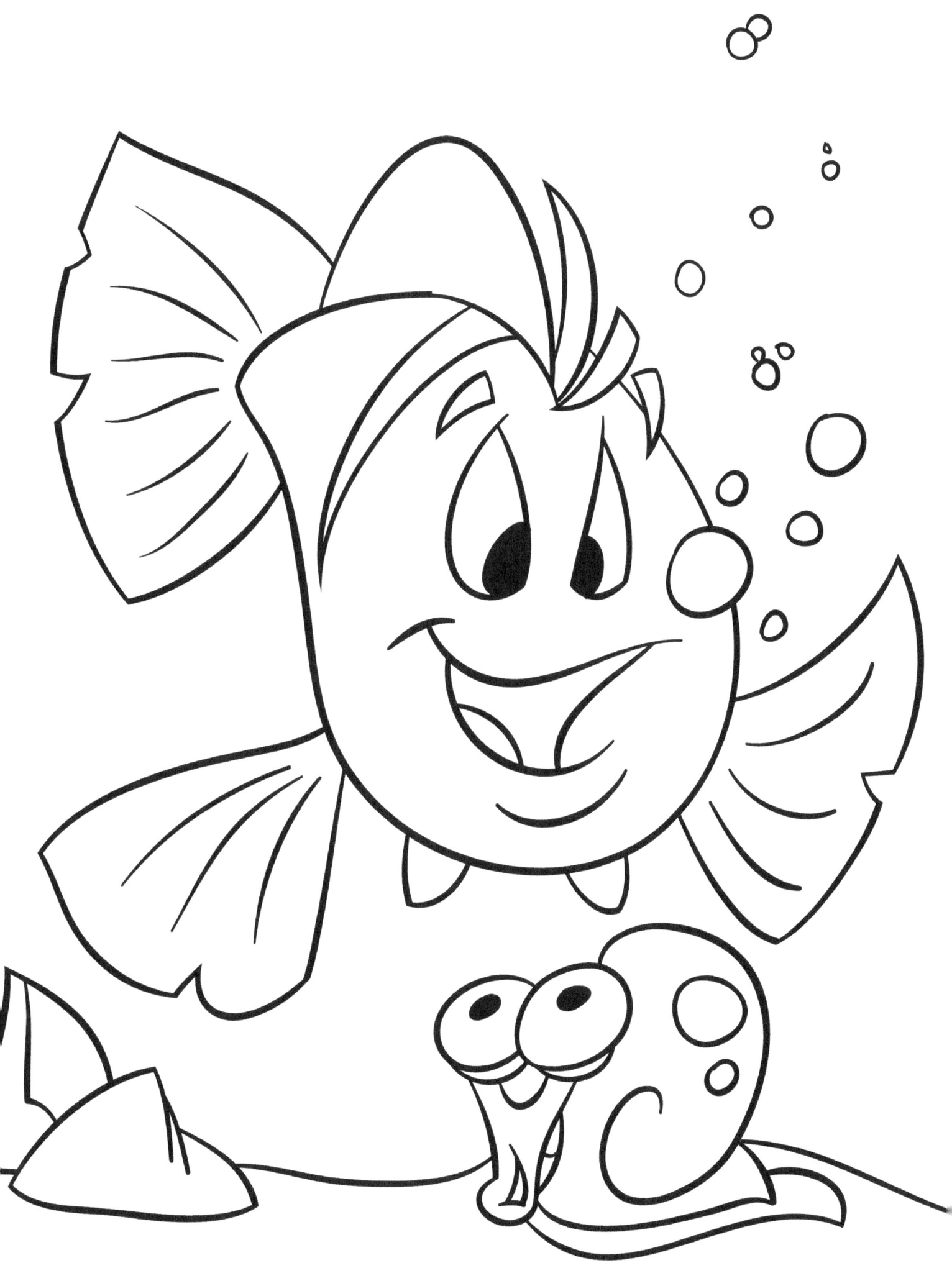

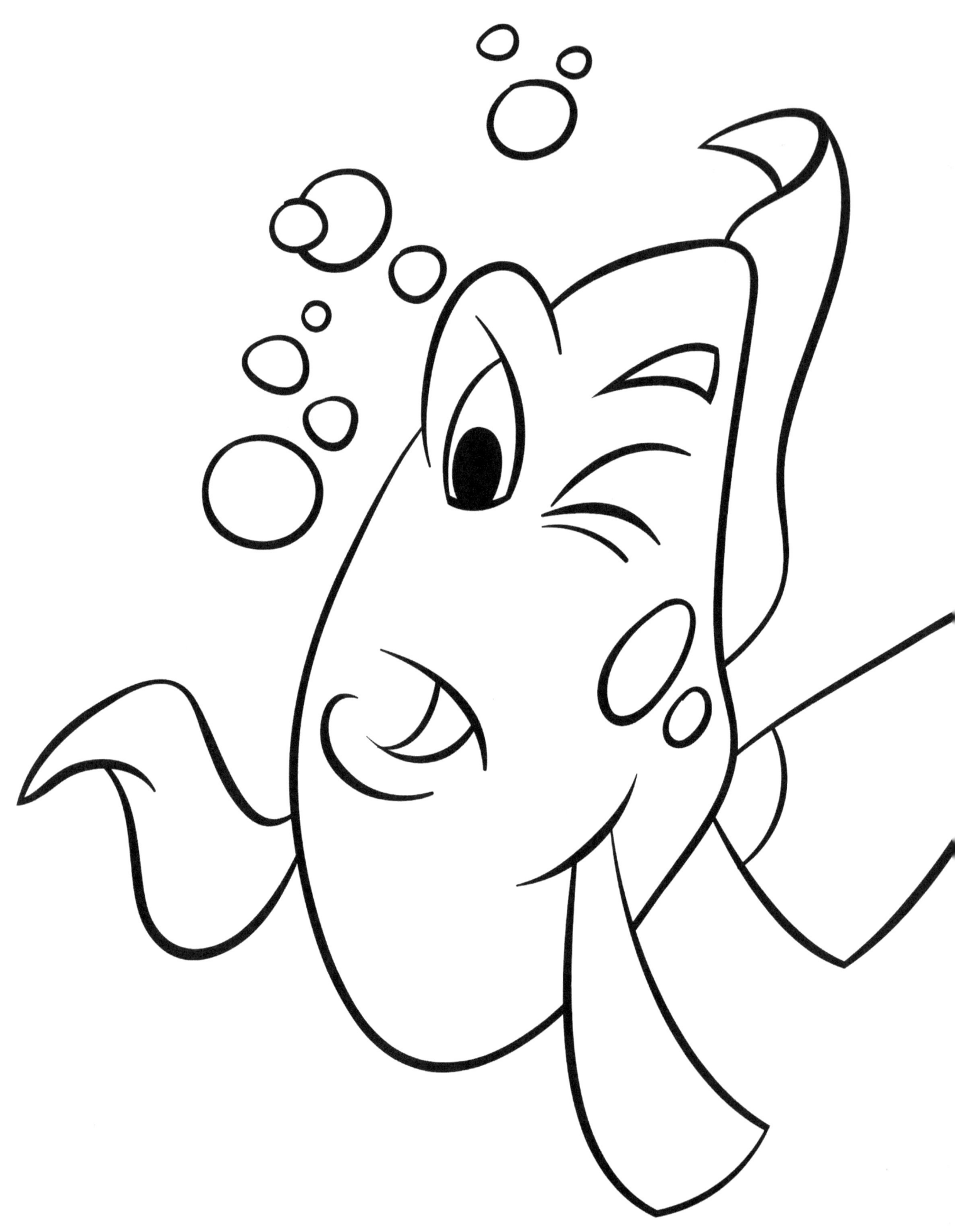

SQUARES

TAKE TURNS, CONNECT A LINE FROM ONE PLANKTON TO ANOTHER. WHOEVER MAKES THE LINE THAT COMPLETES THE BOX PUTS THEIR INITALS INSID THAT BOX. THE PERSON WITH THE MOST SQUARES AT THE END OF THE GAME WINS!

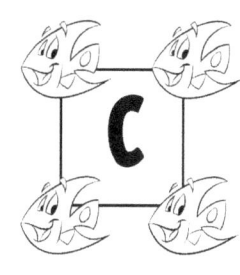

EXAMPLE

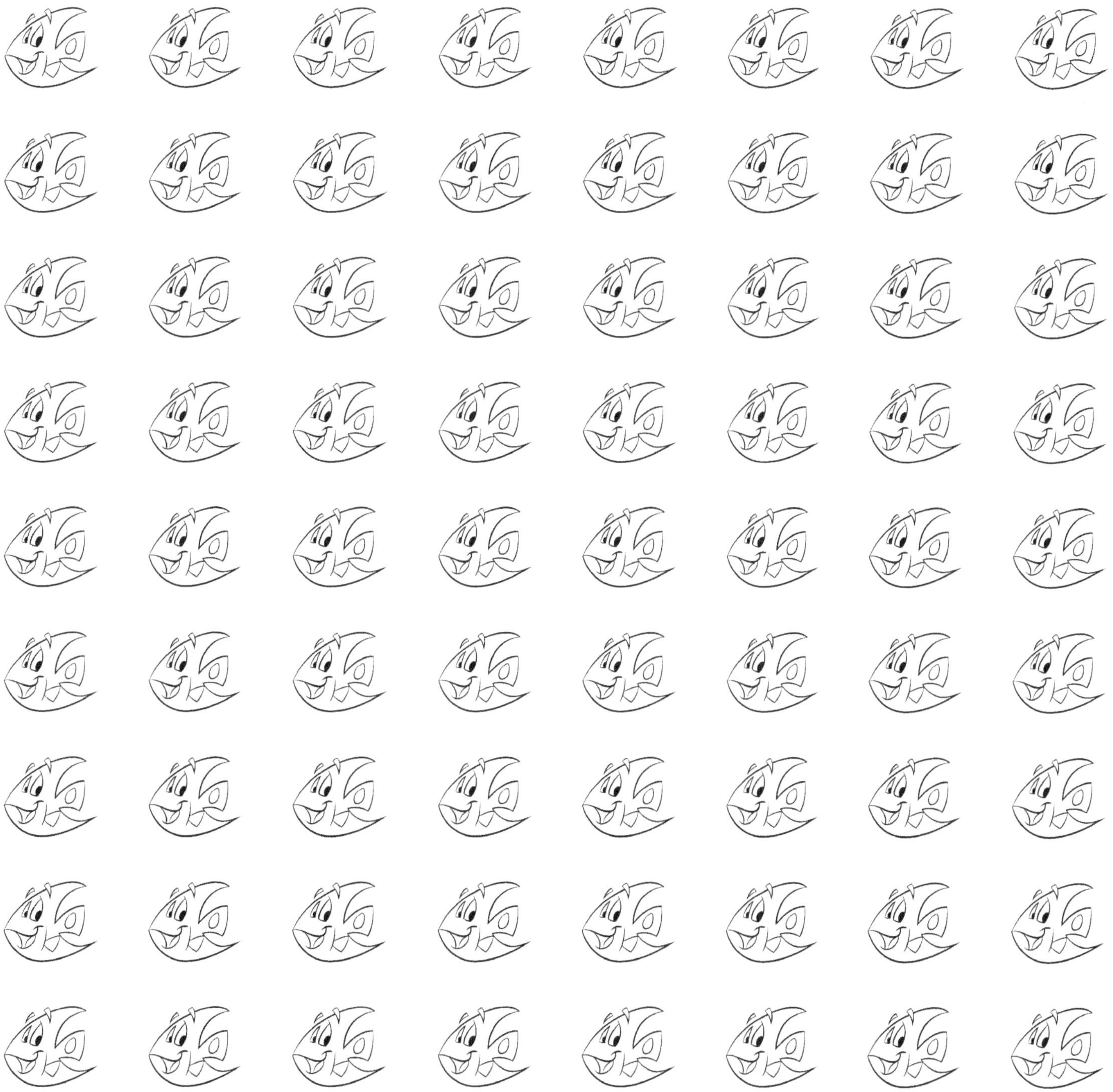

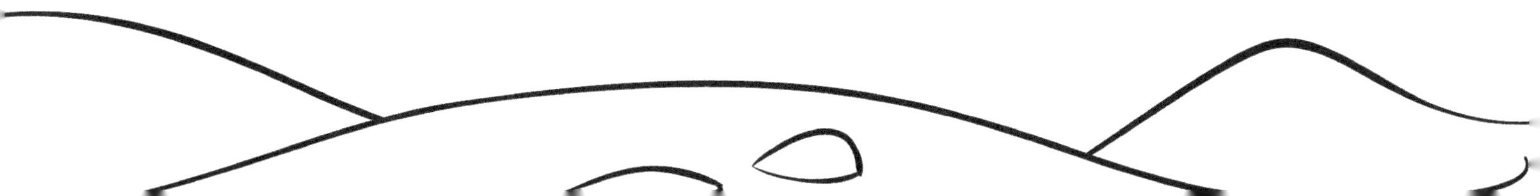

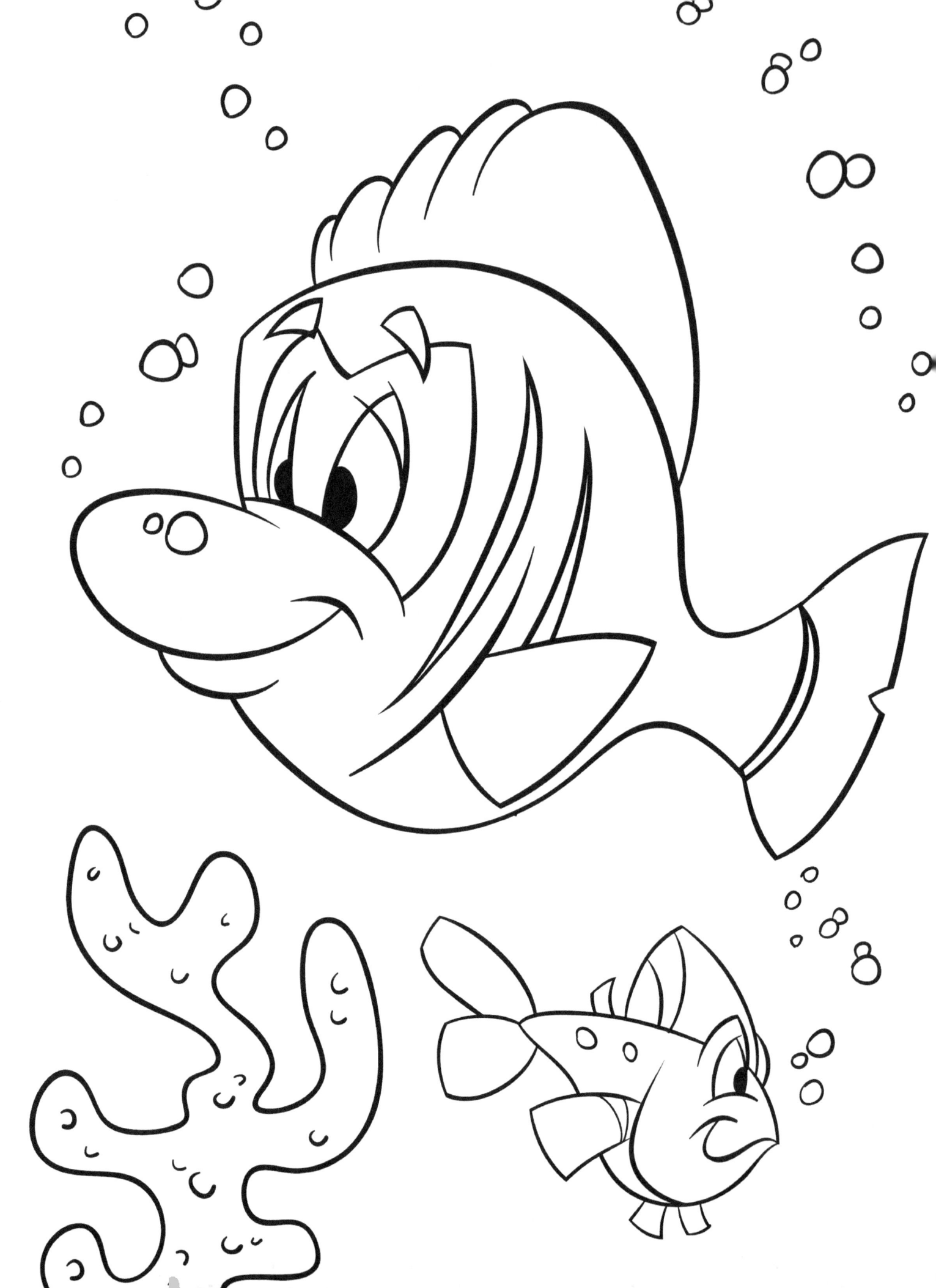

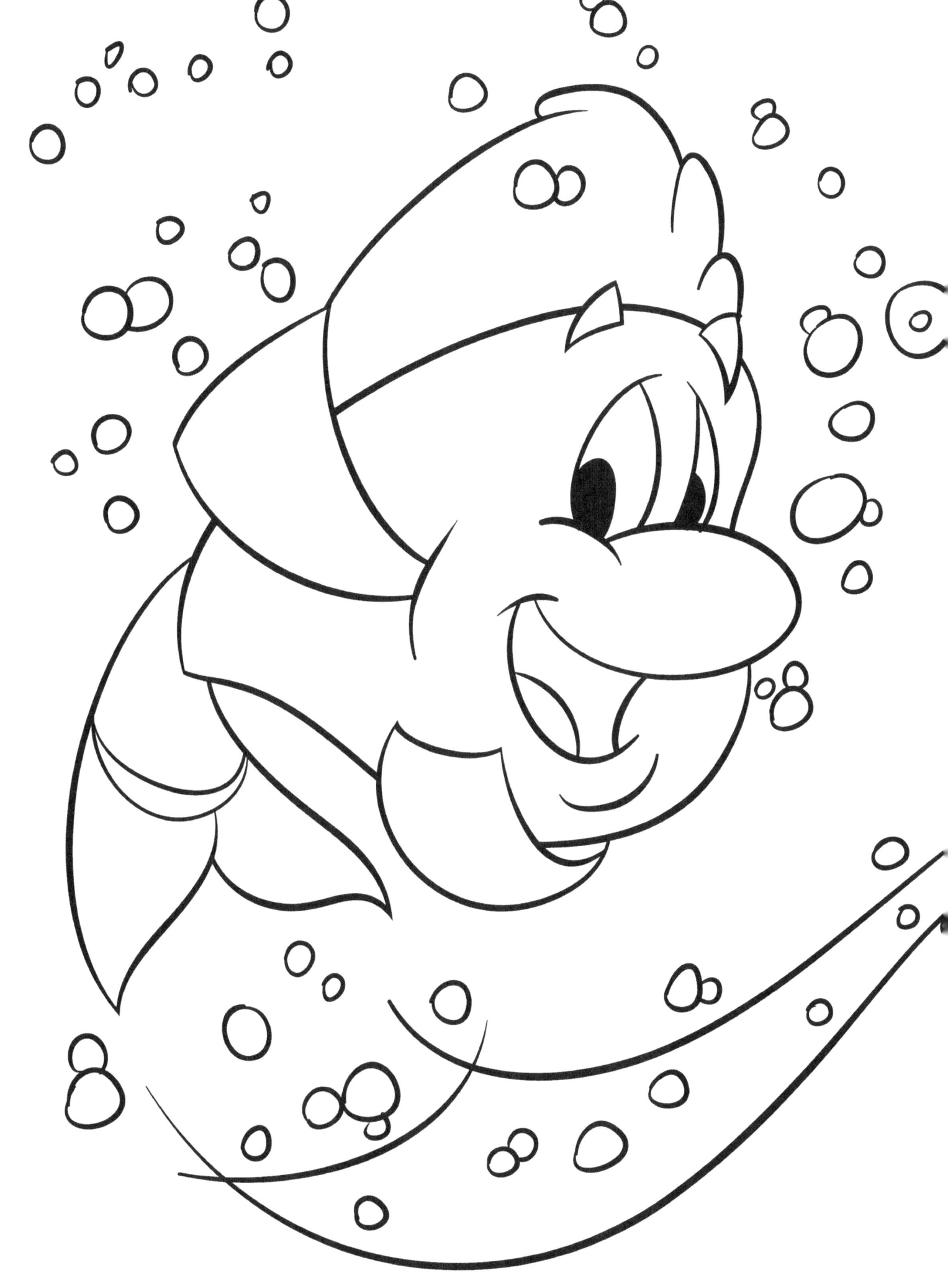

HOW MANY?

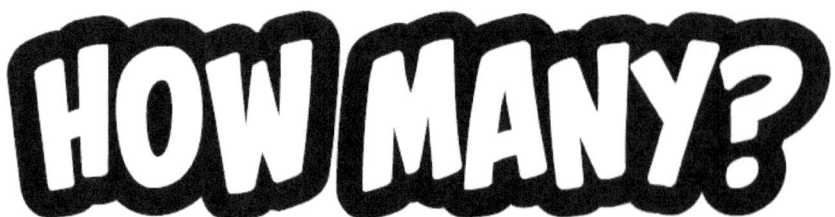

HOW MANY WORDS CAN YOU MAKE USING THE LETTERS BELOW.

AQUARIUM SEA LIFE

EXAMPLE: IF

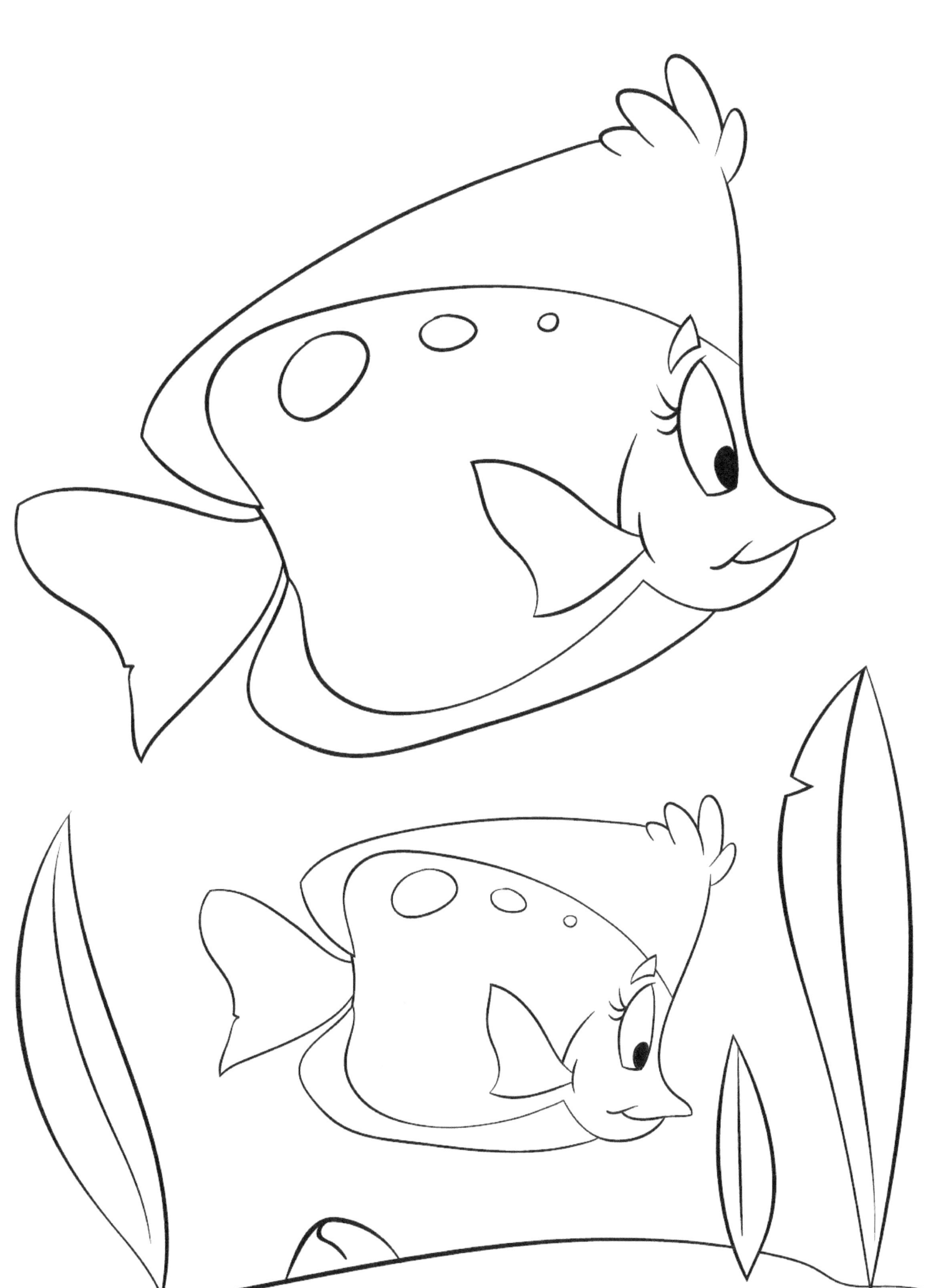

FIND THE DIFFERENT PICTURE

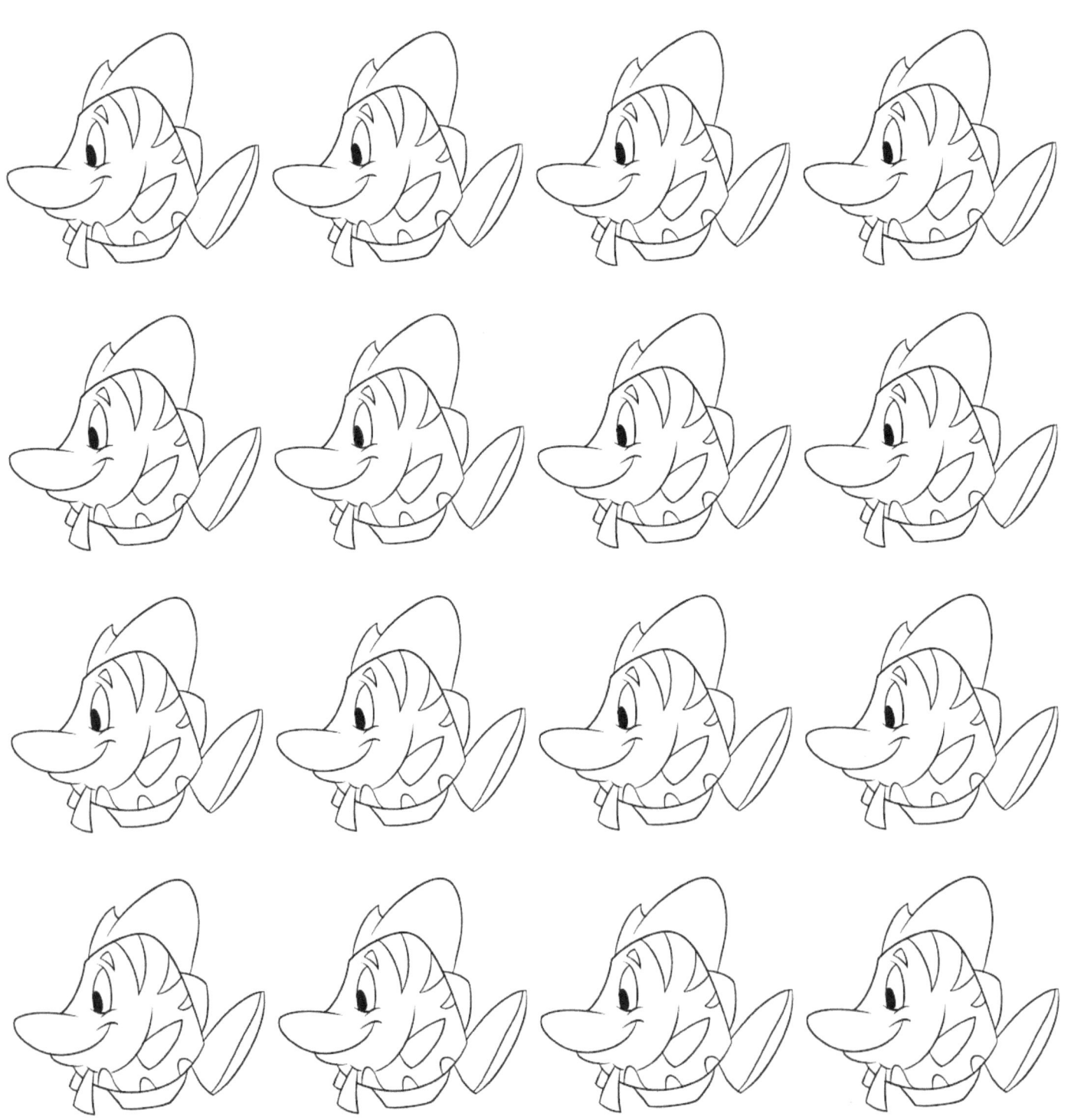

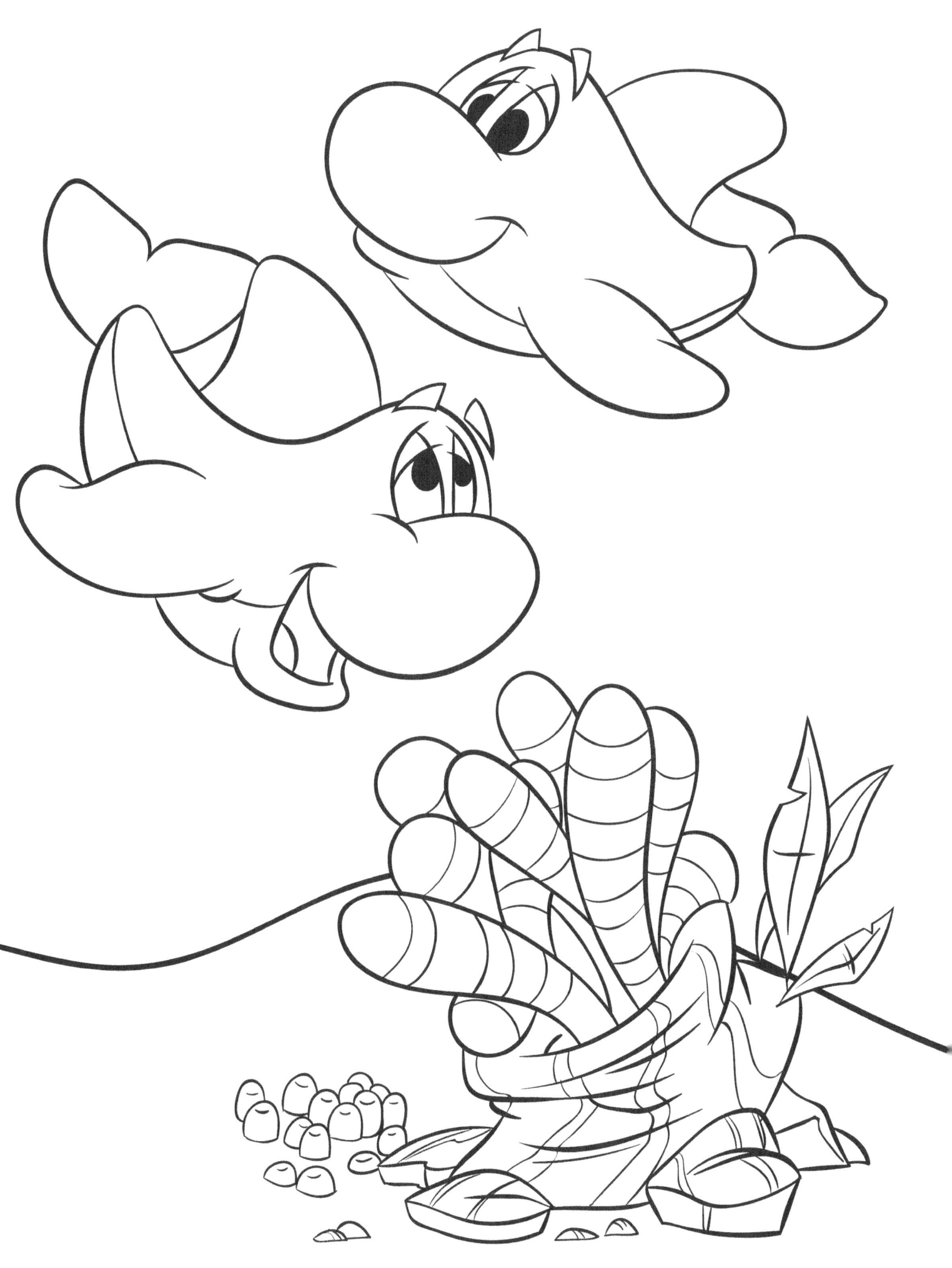

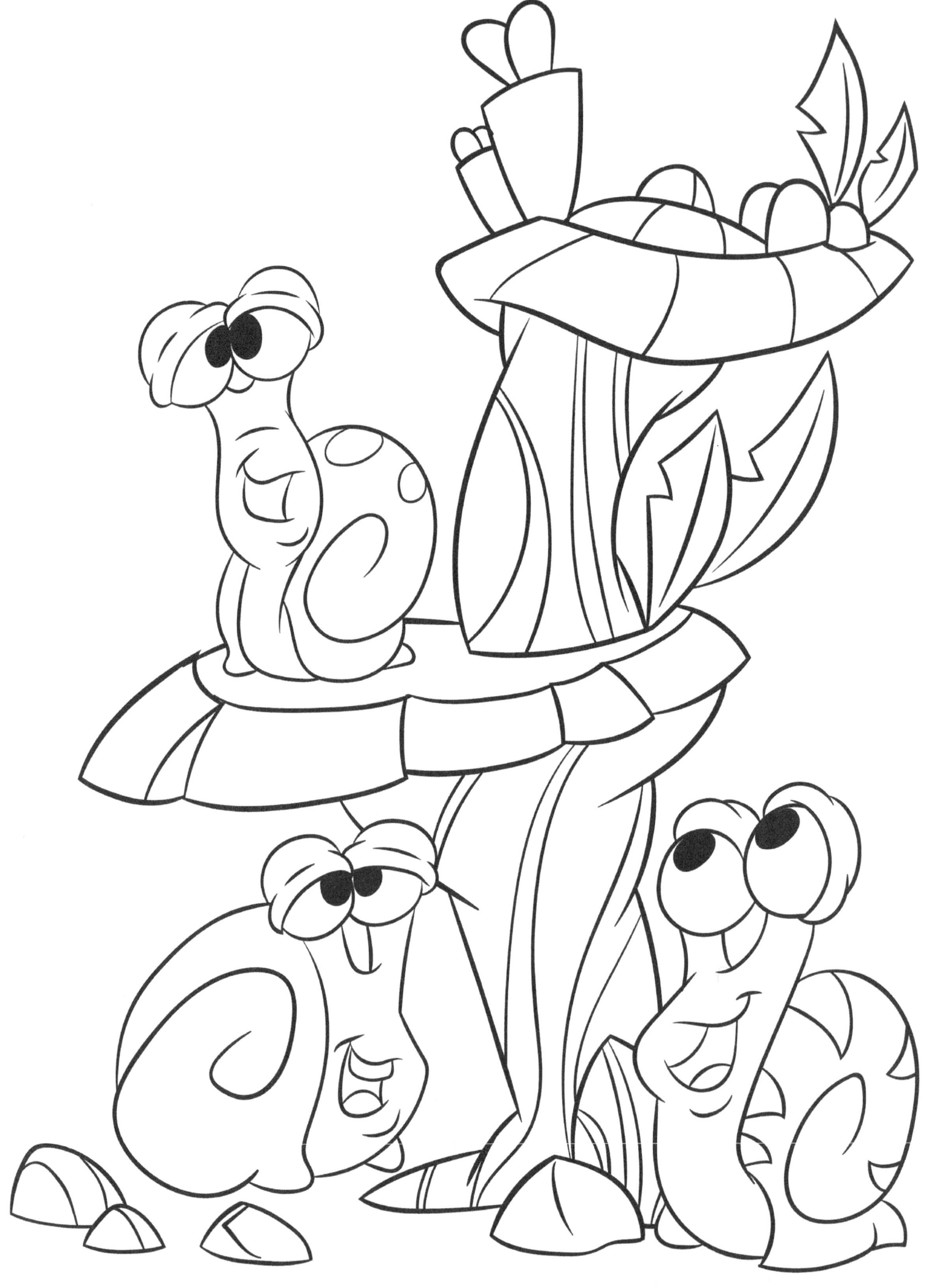

TIC-TAC-TOE

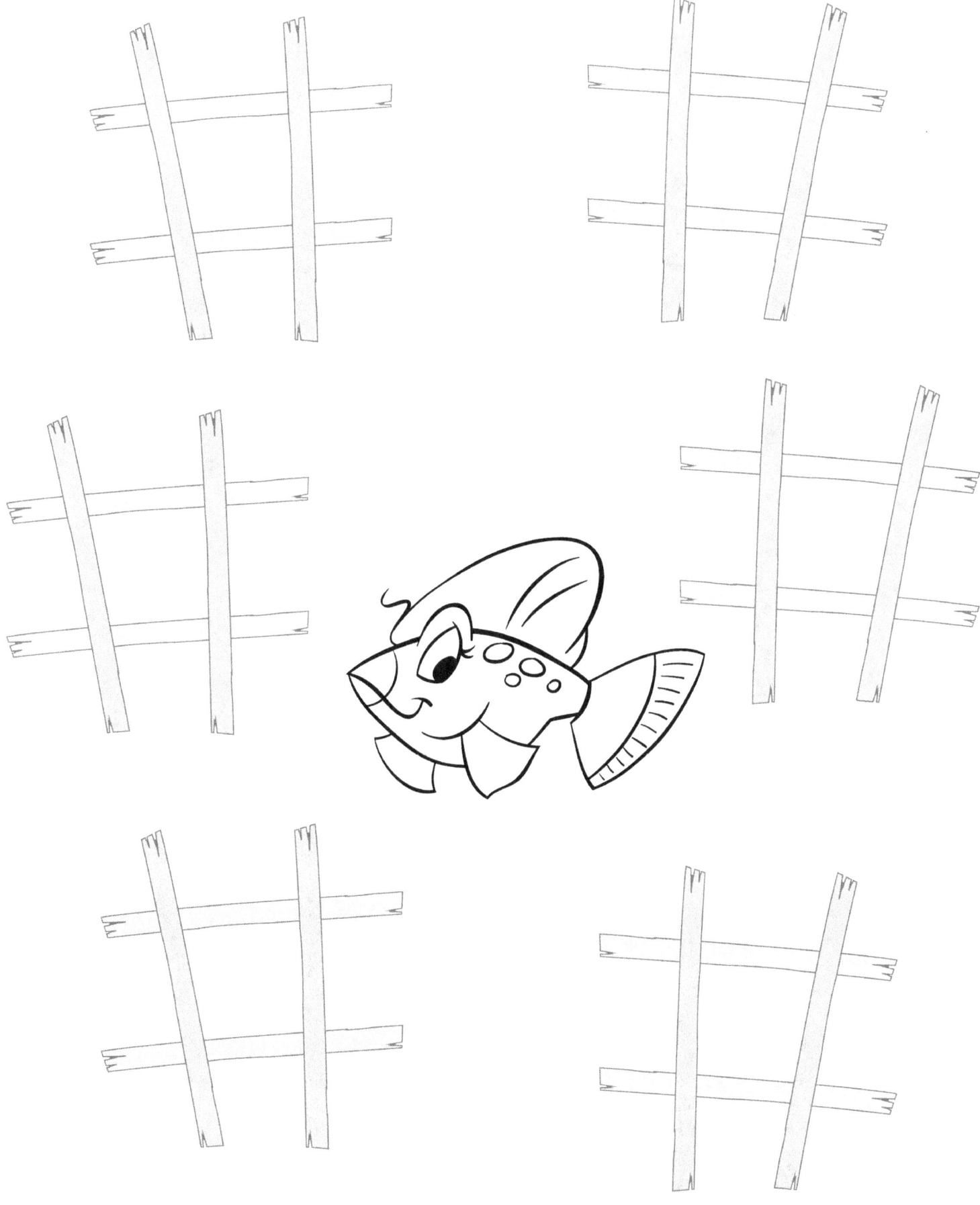

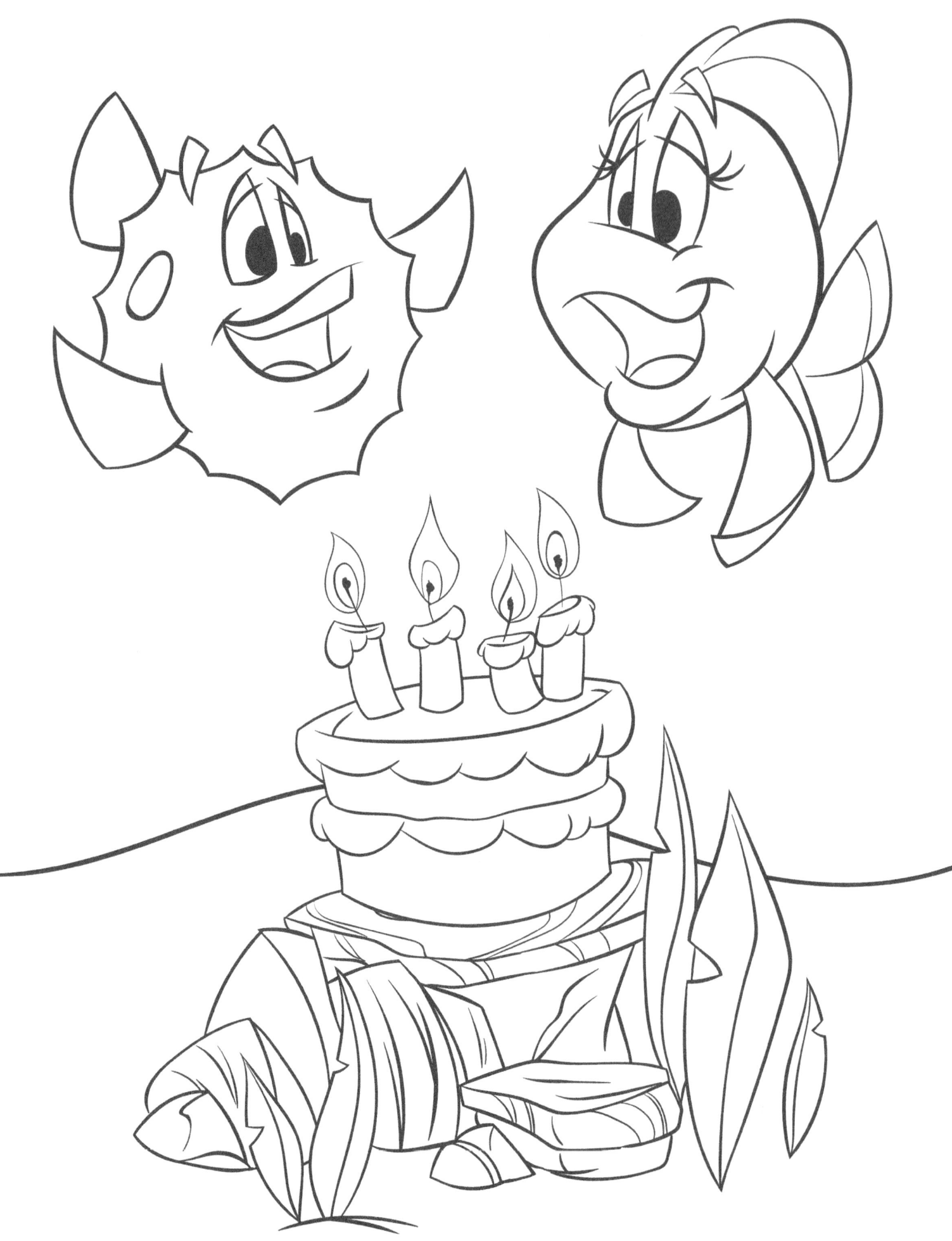

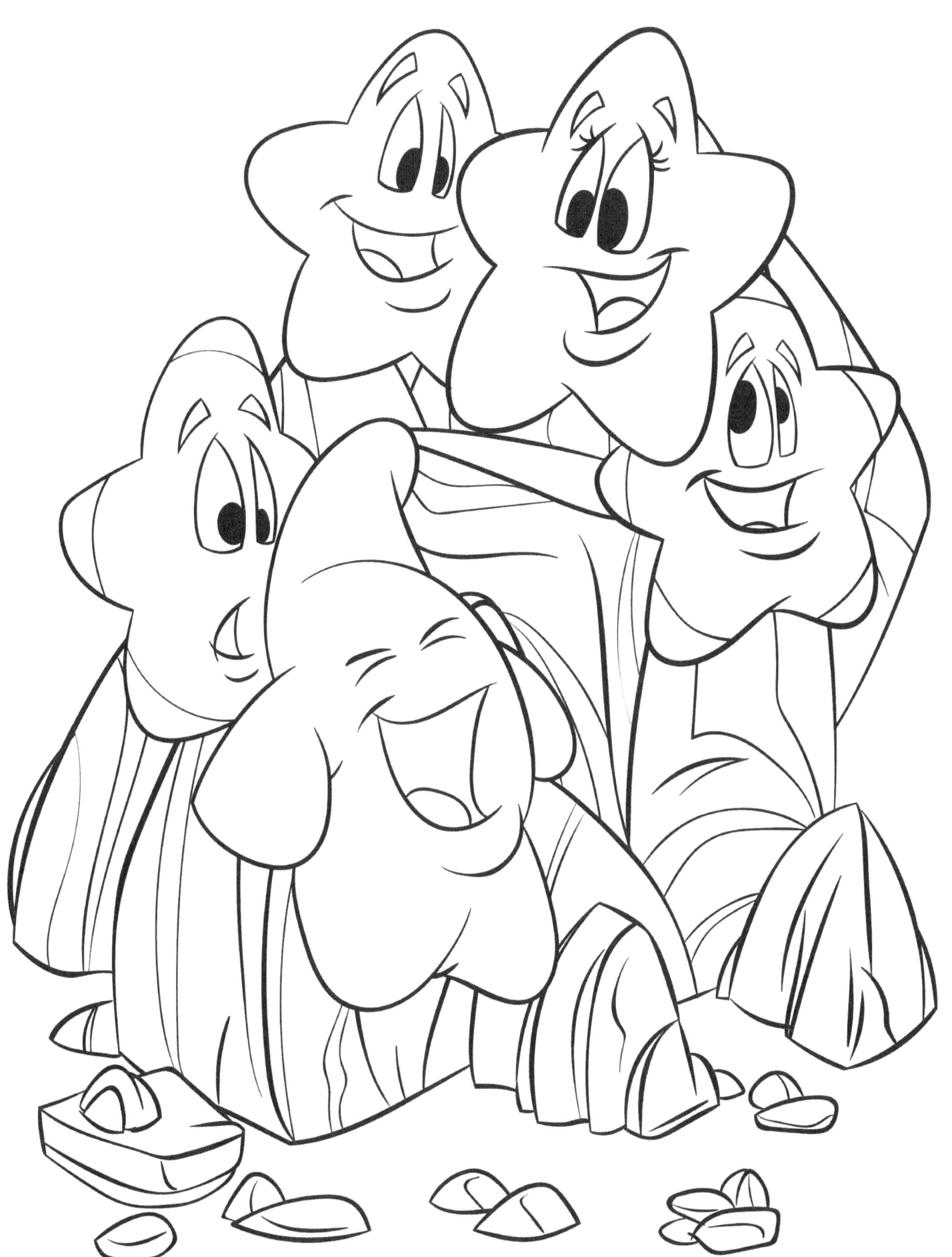

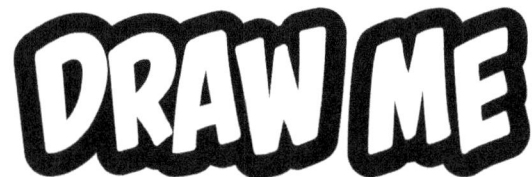

USE THE GRID TO HELP
YOU DRAW THIS FISH.

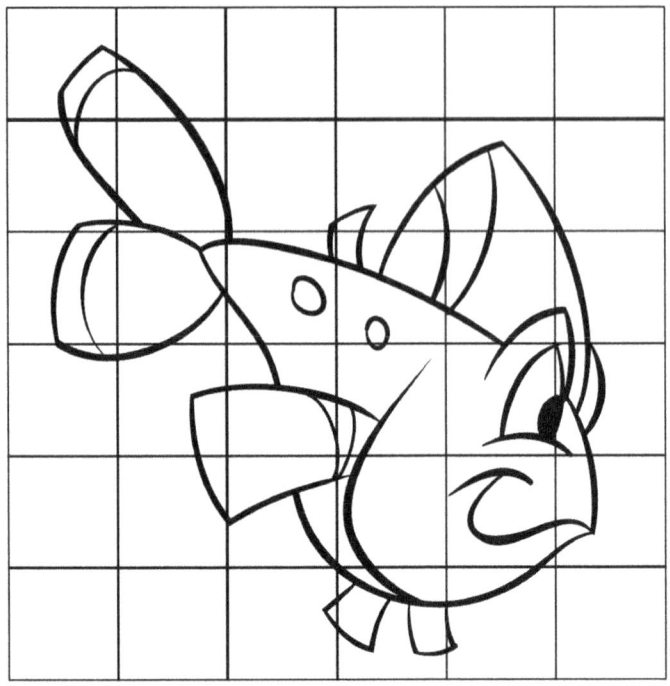

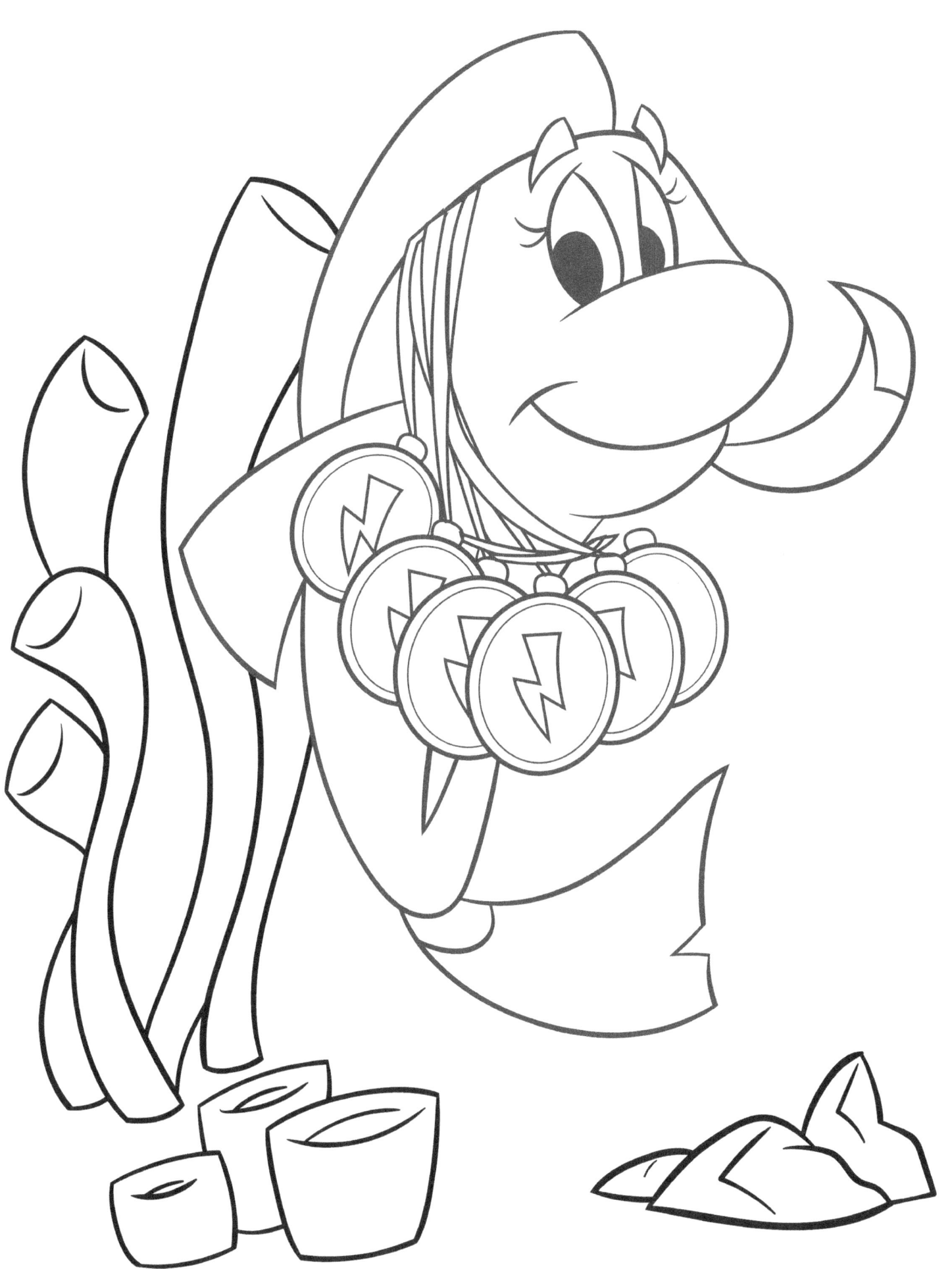

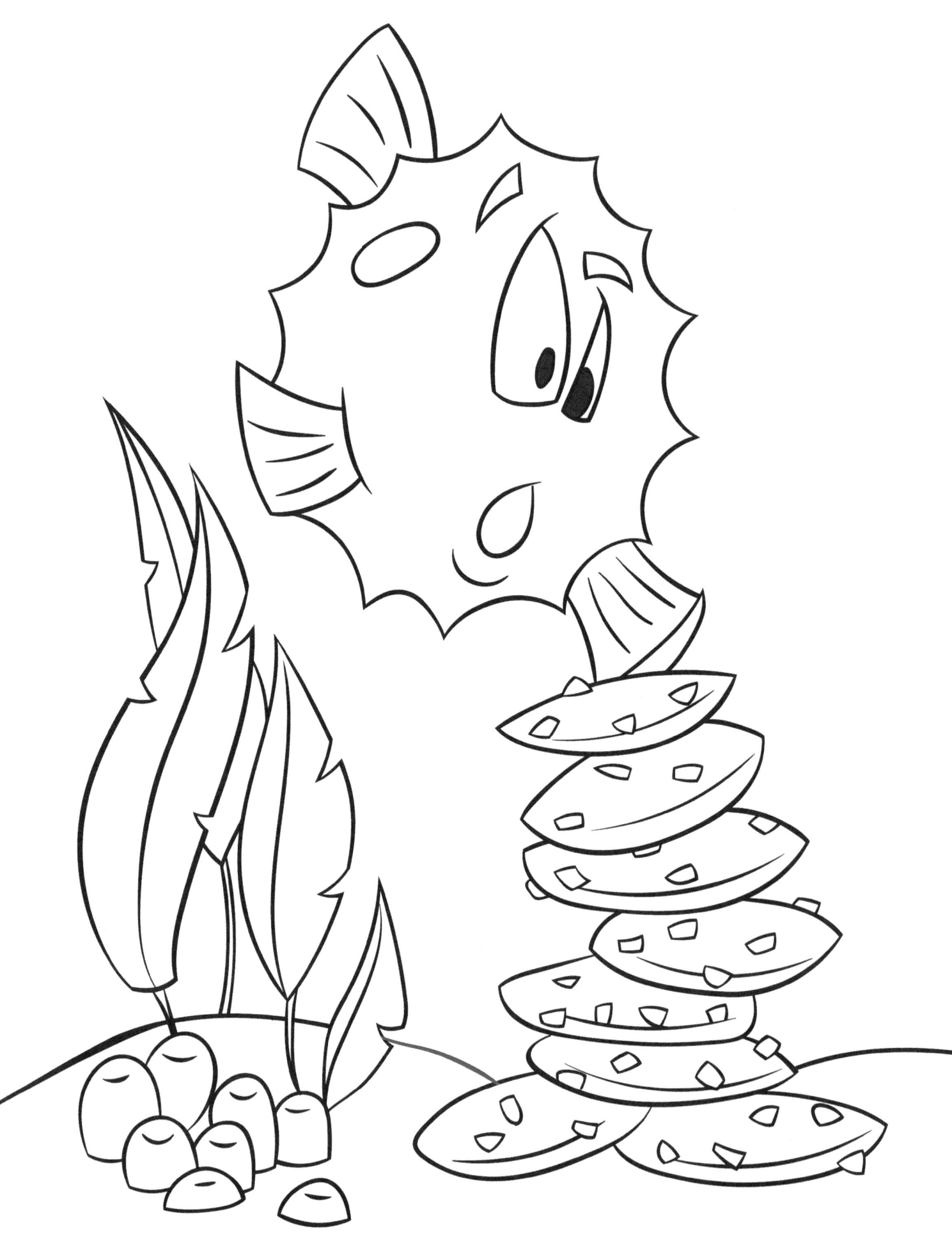

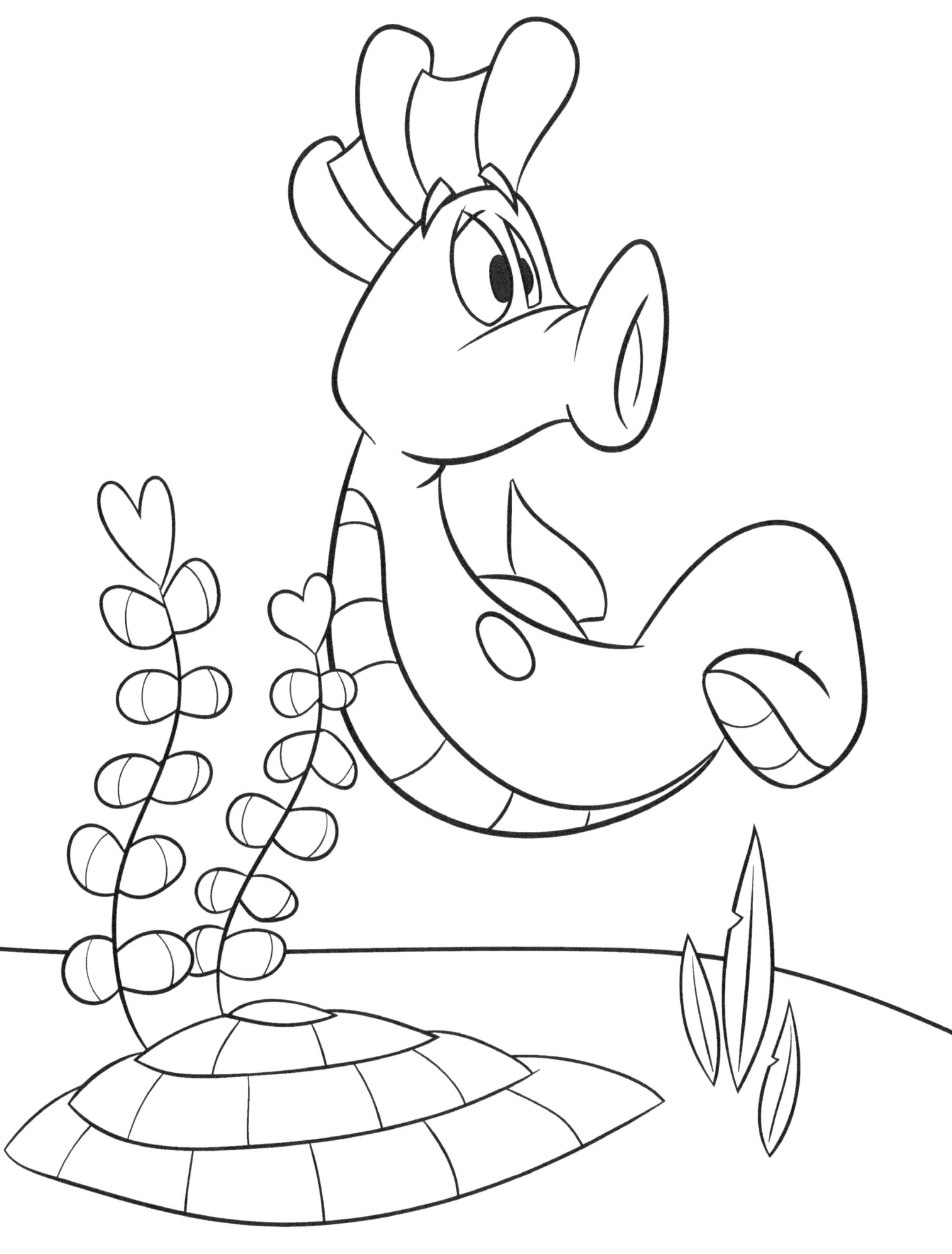

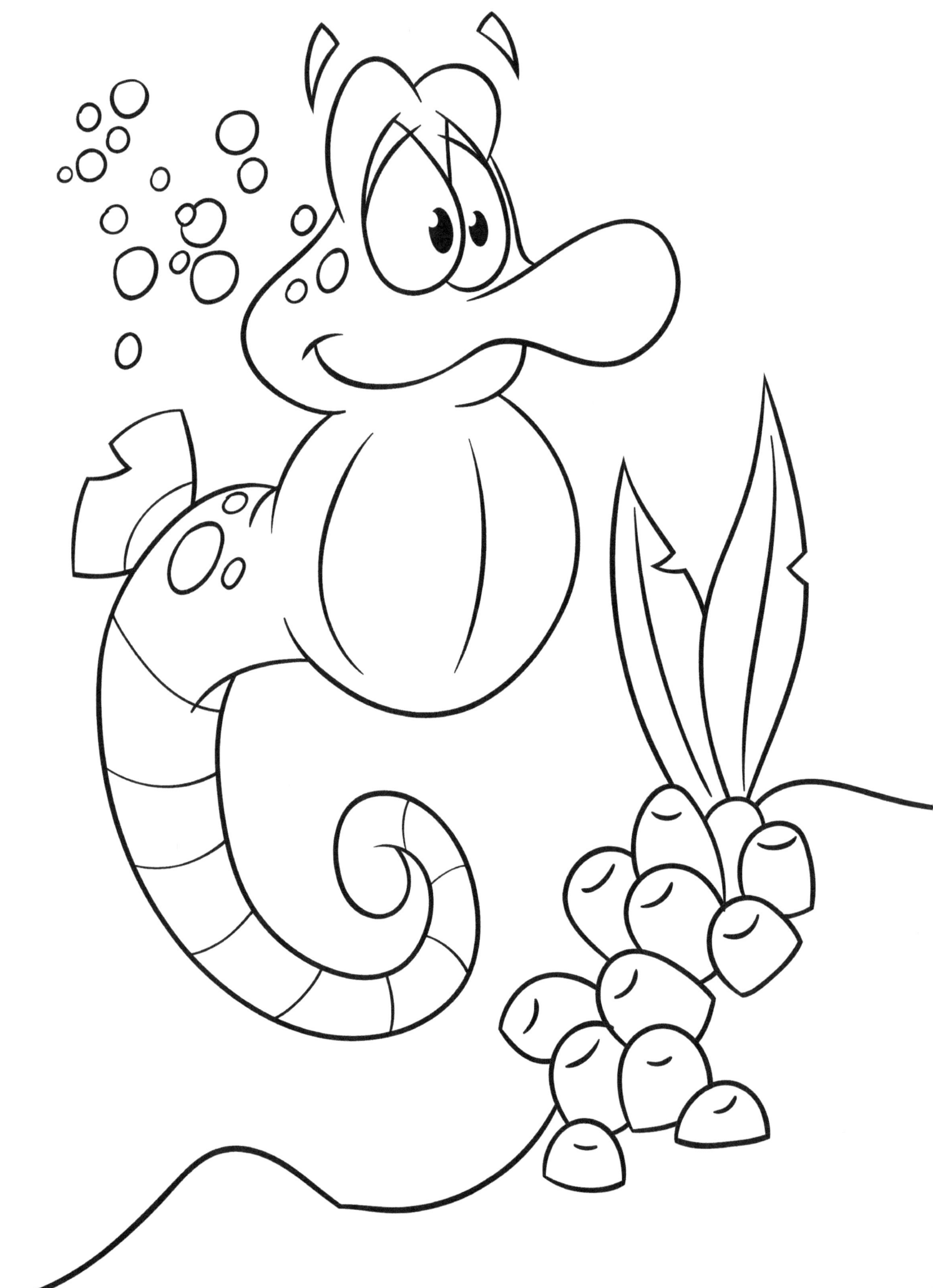

Find the Different Picture

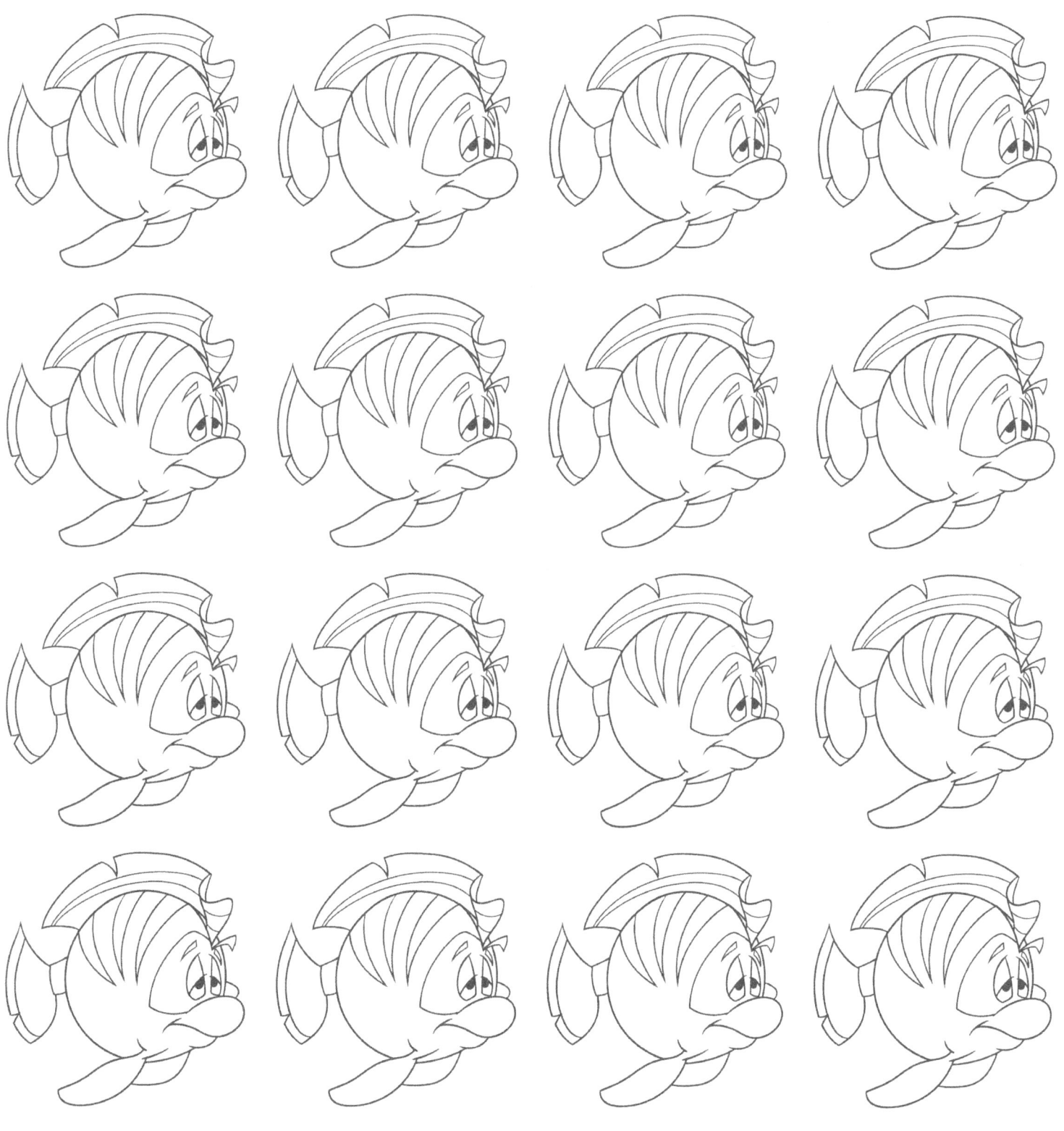

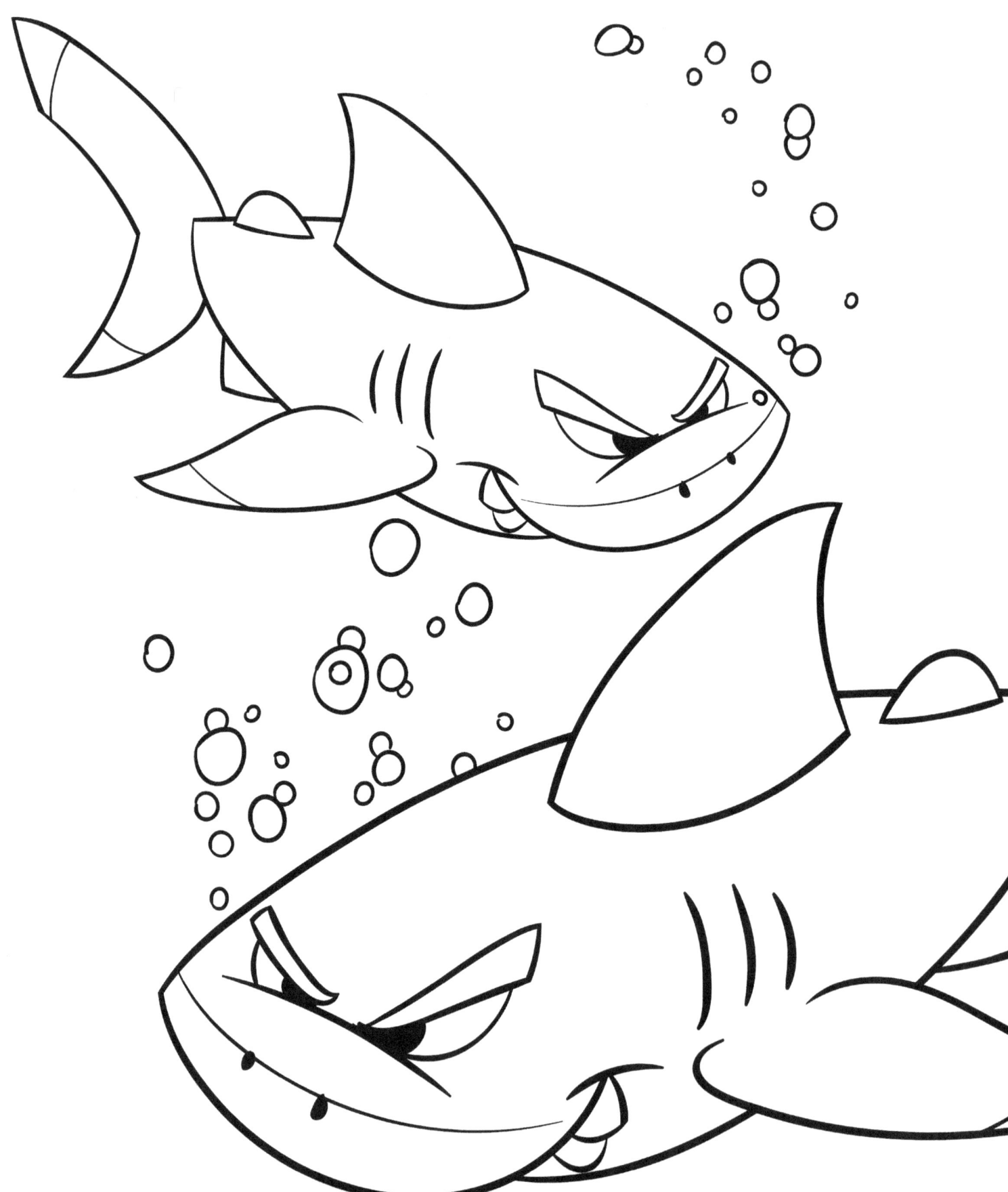

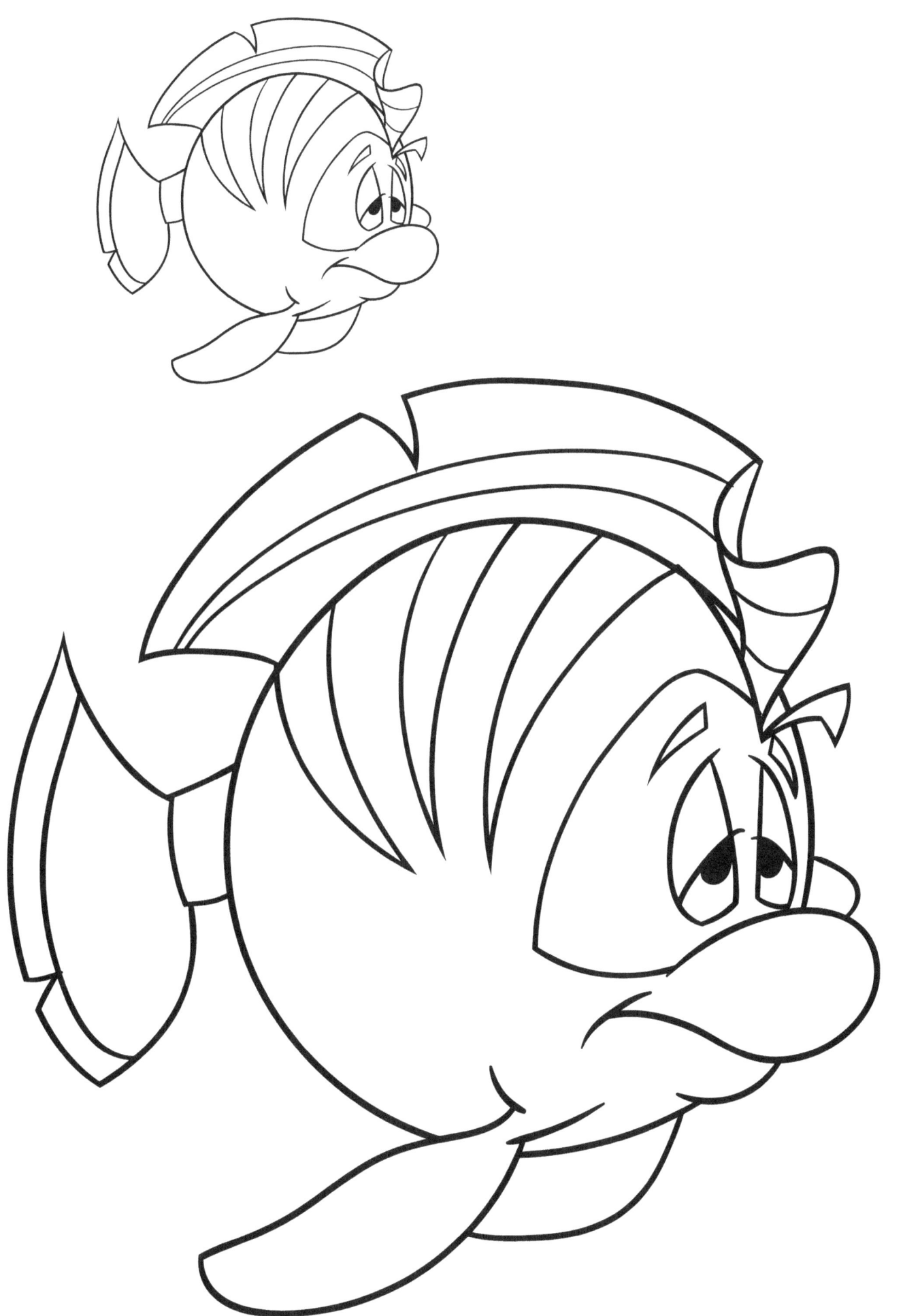

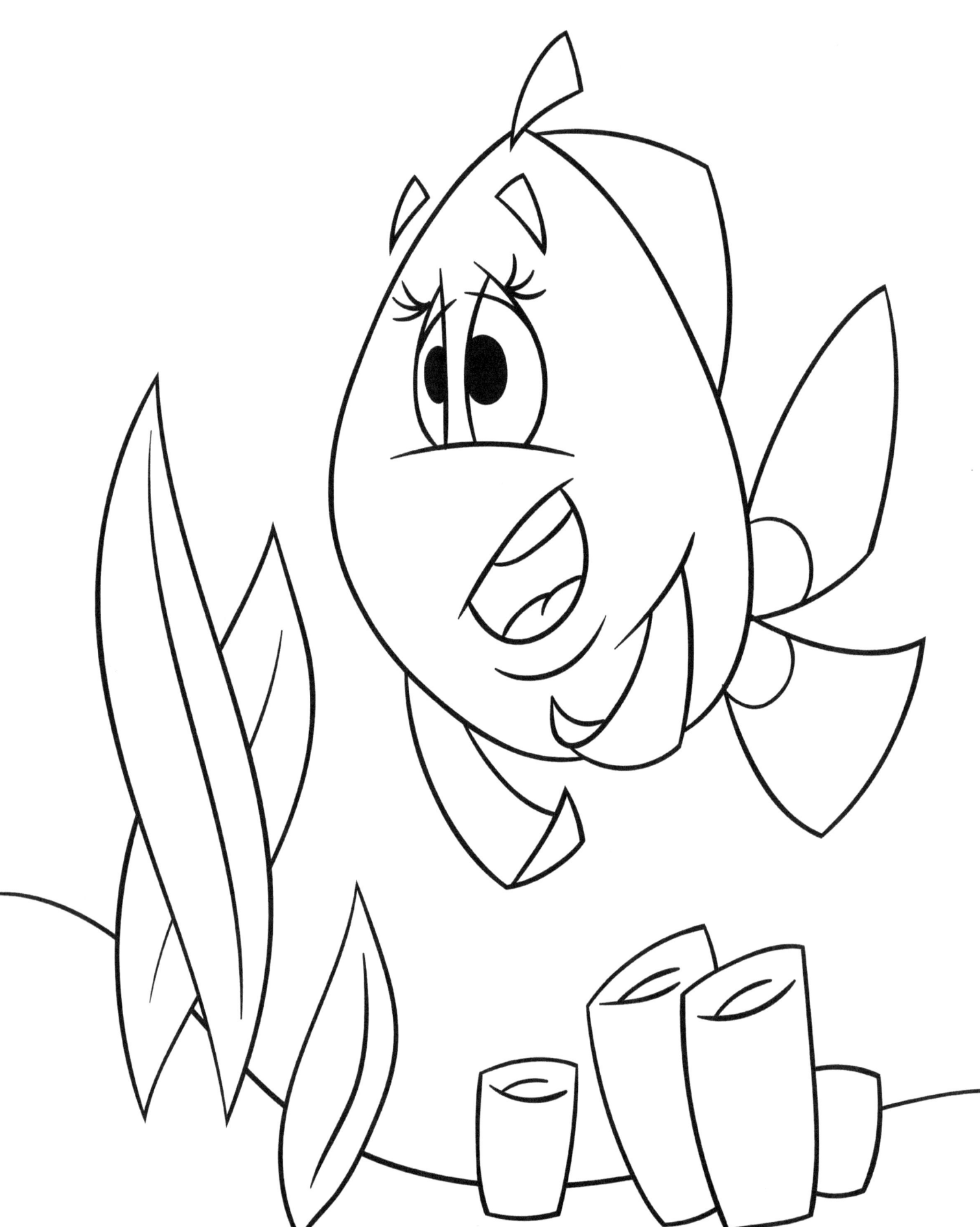

TIC-TAC-TOE

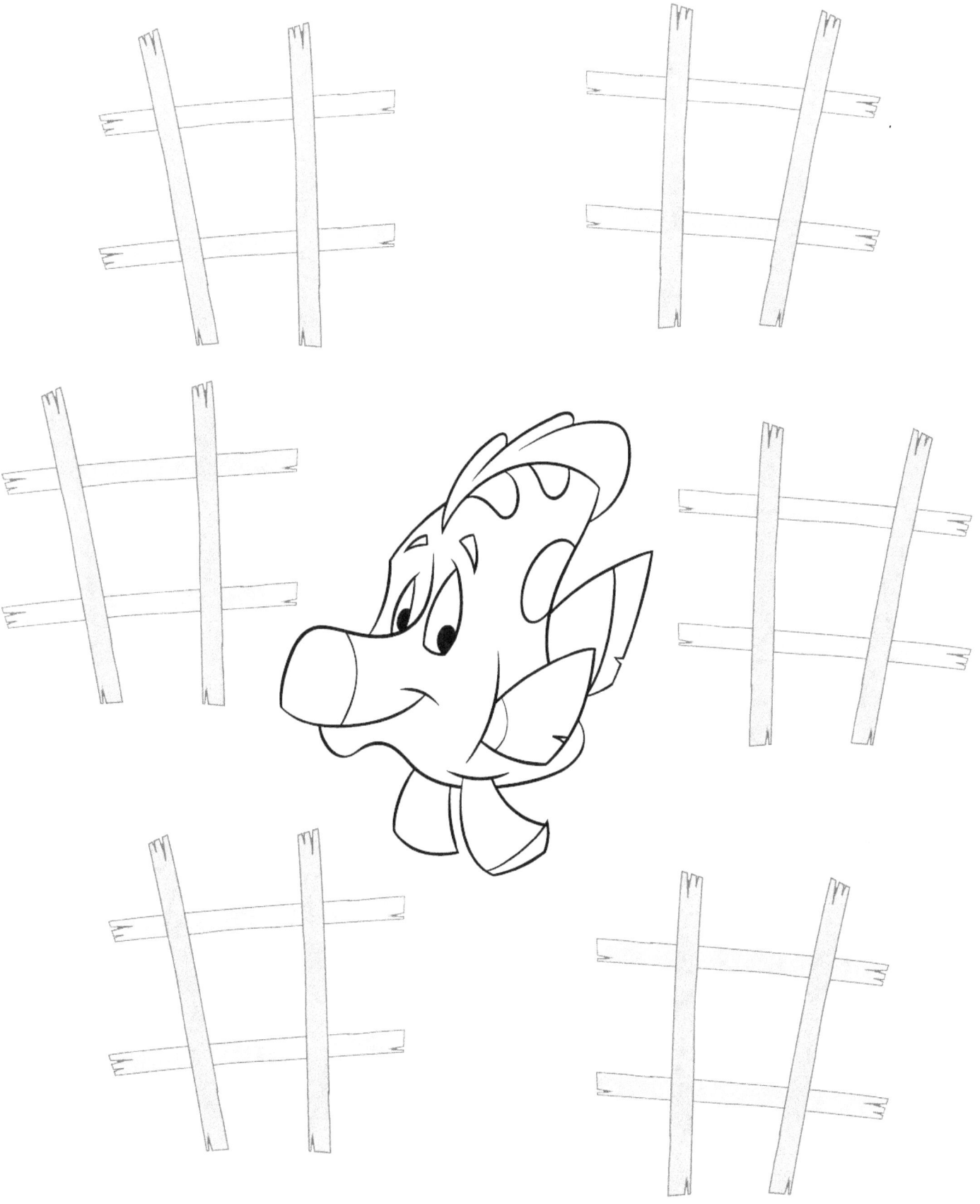

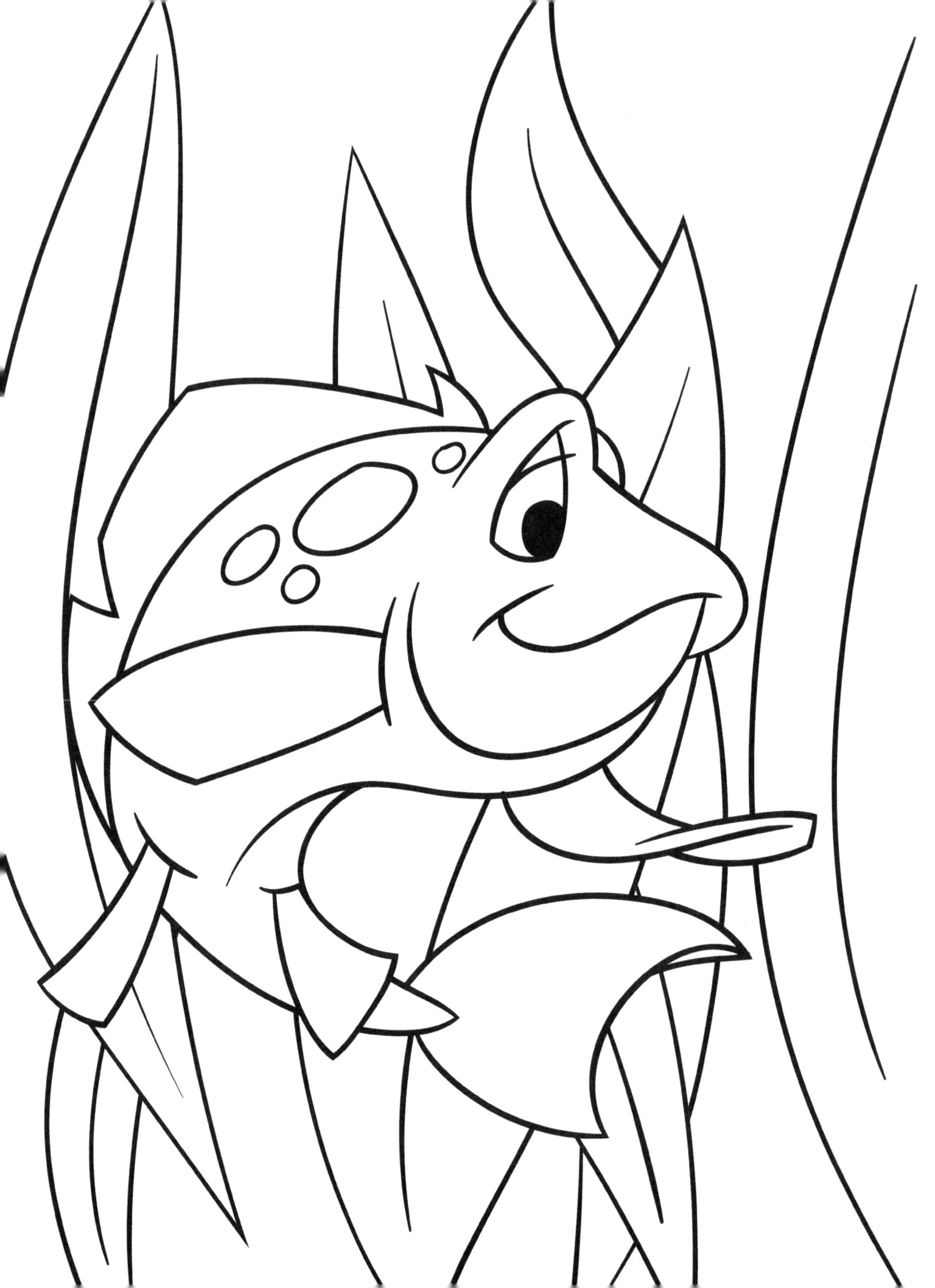

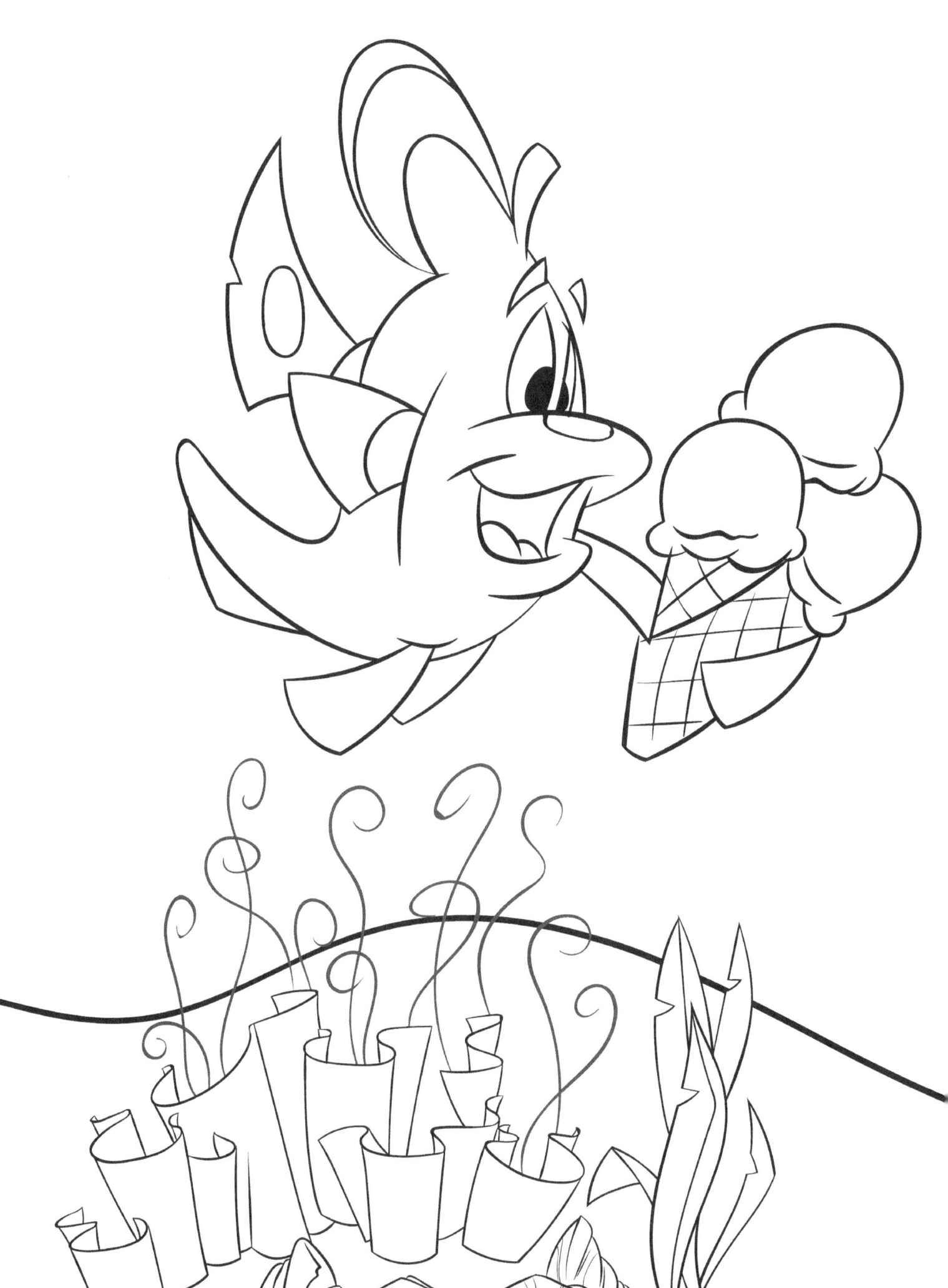

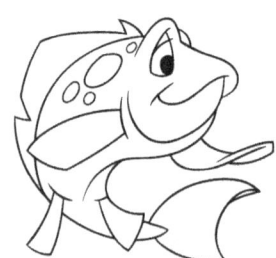
FIND YOUR WAY OUT
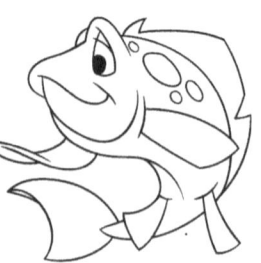

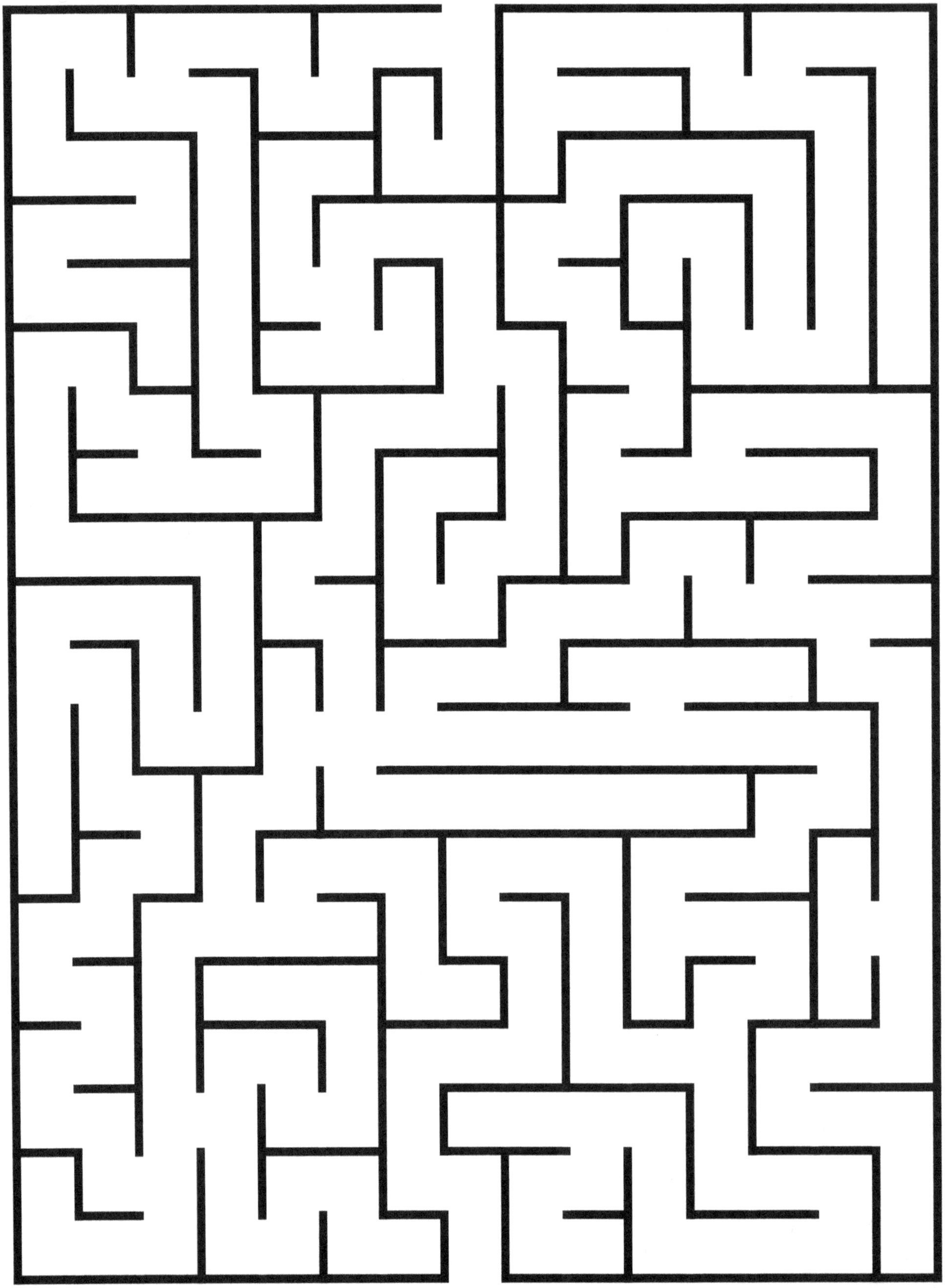

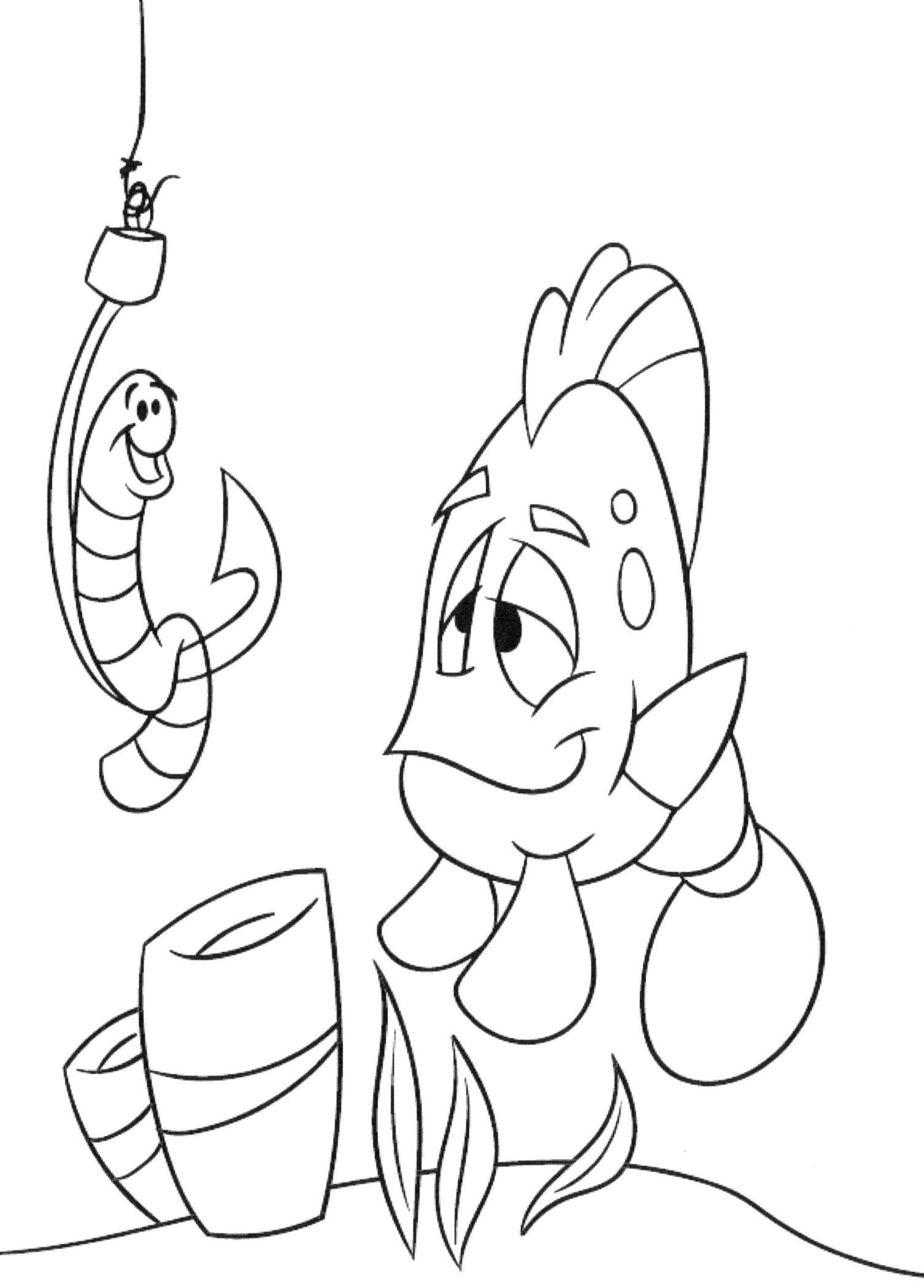

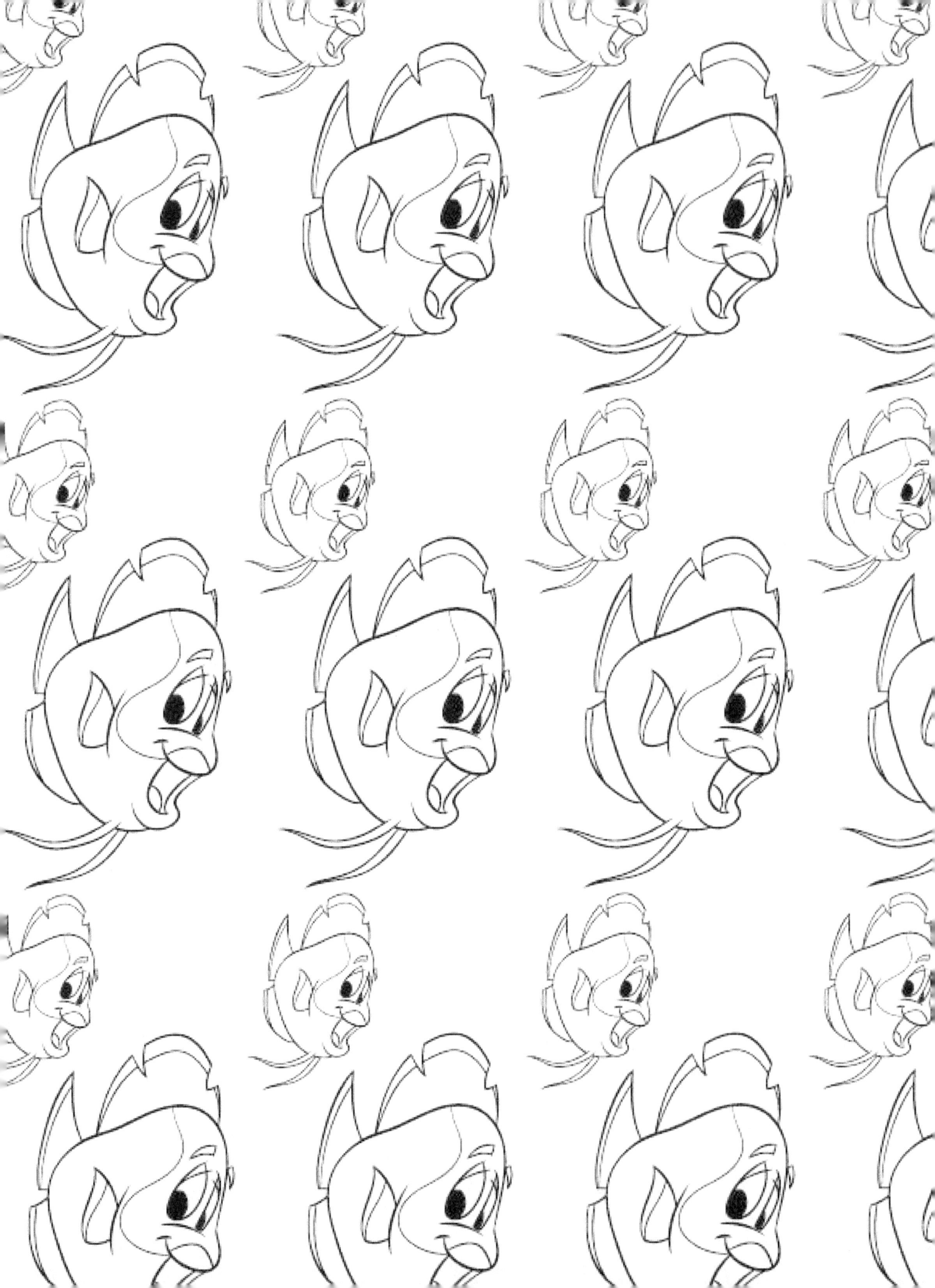

MATCH THE SHADOW

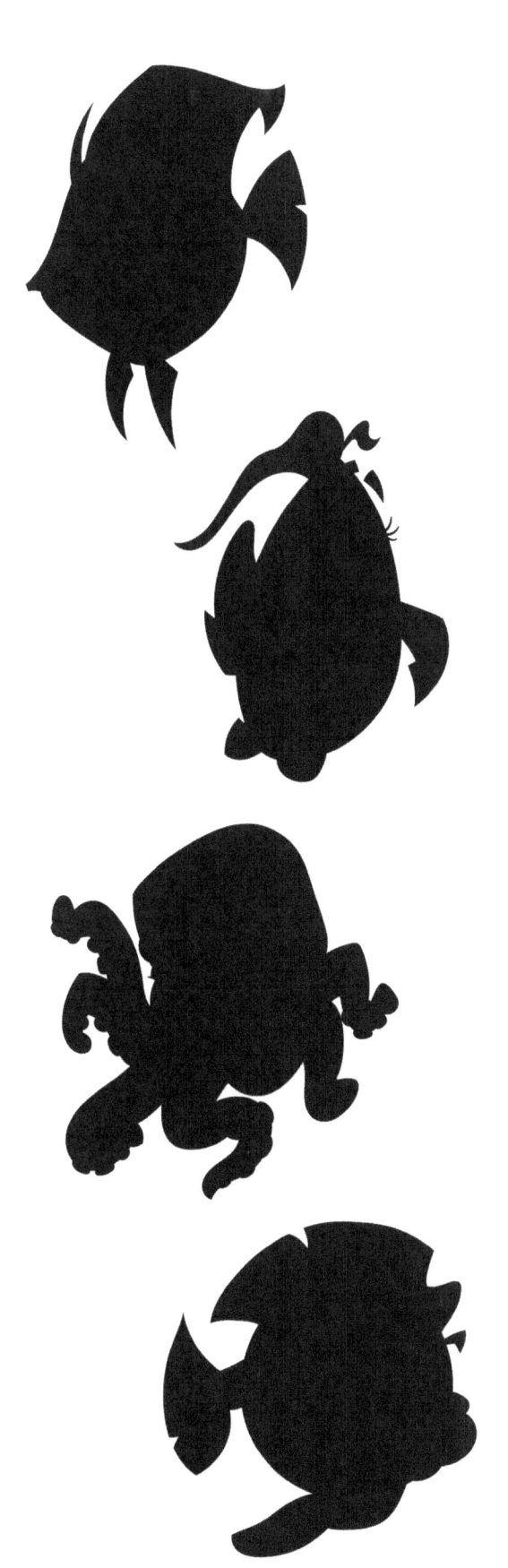
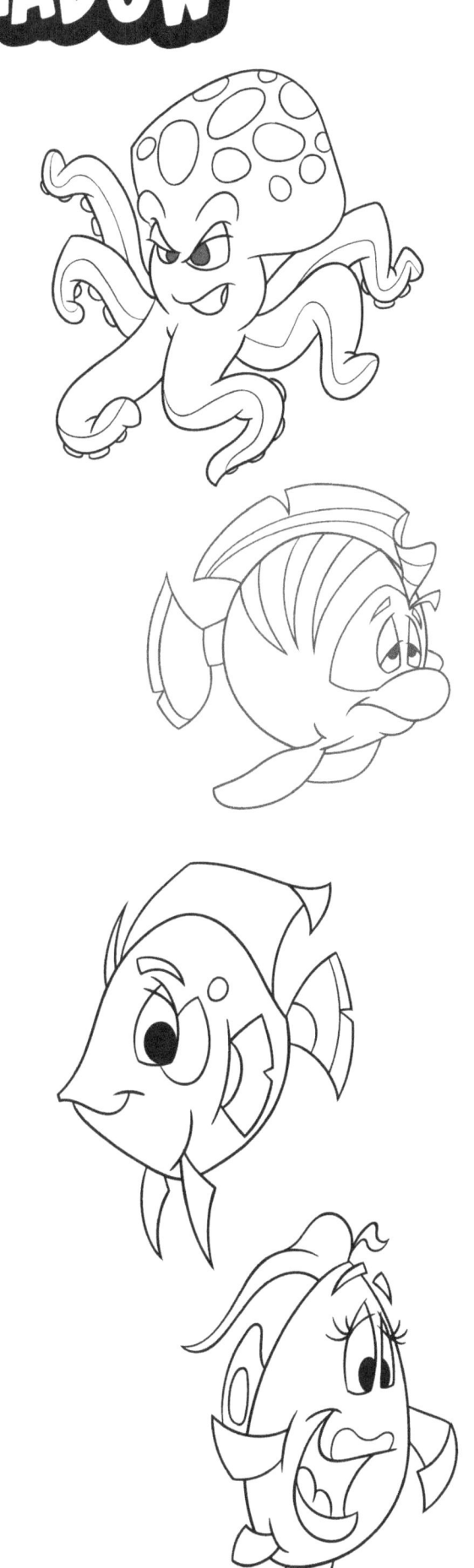

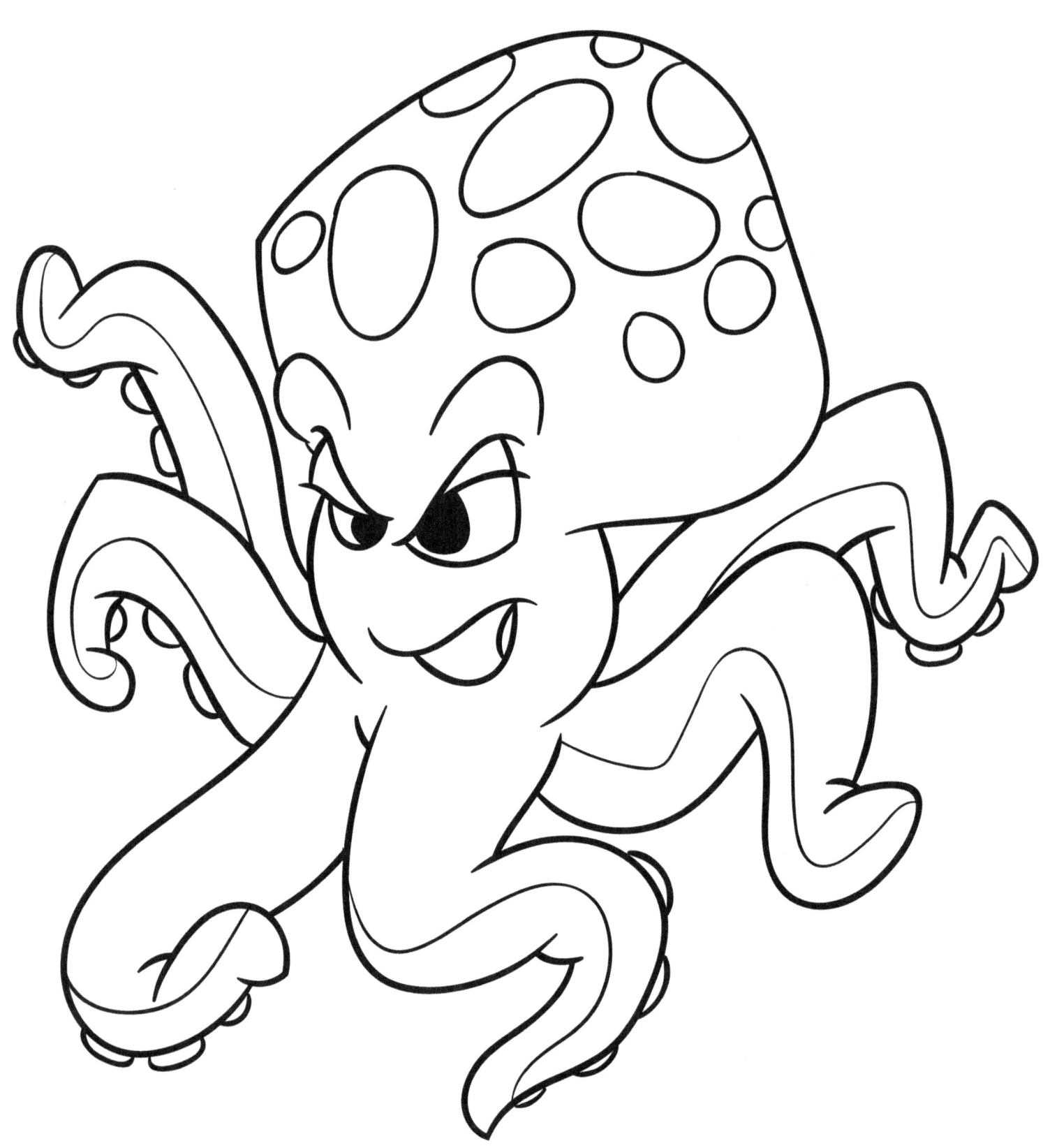

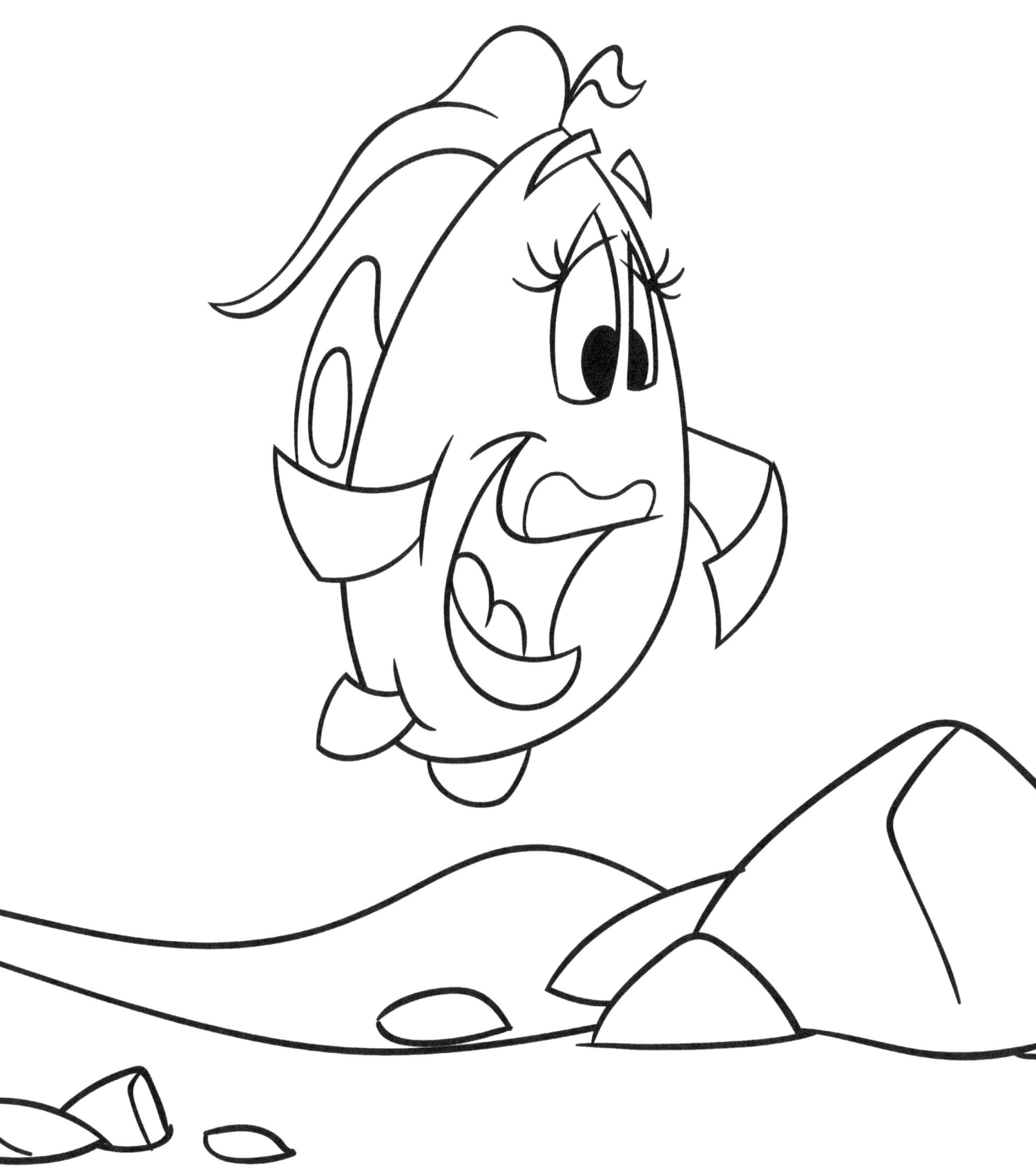

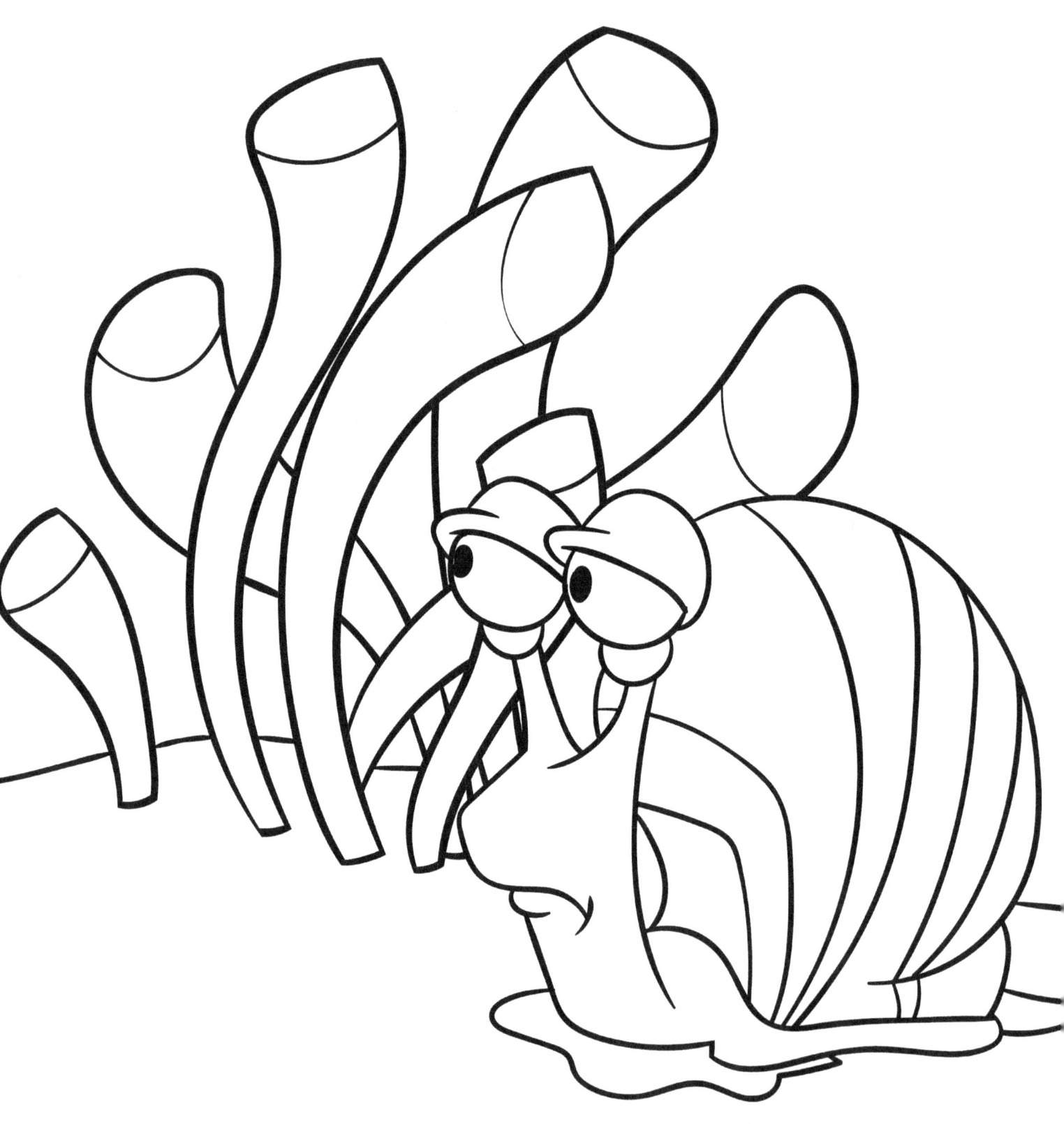

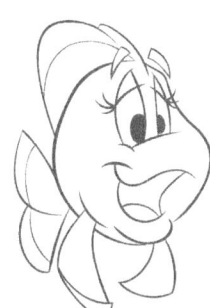 # FIND YOUR WAY OUT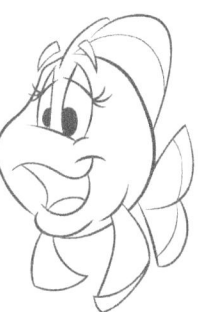

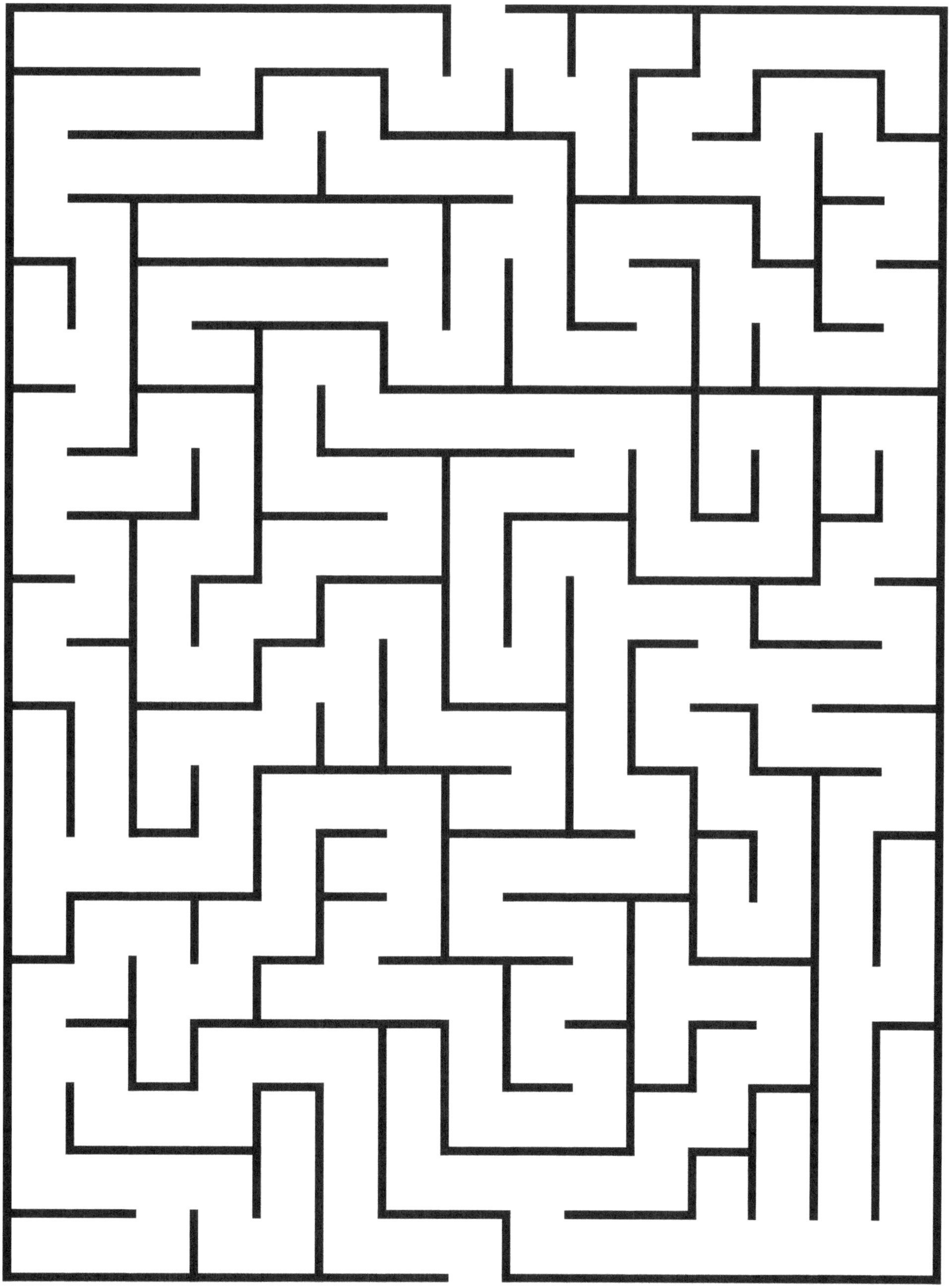

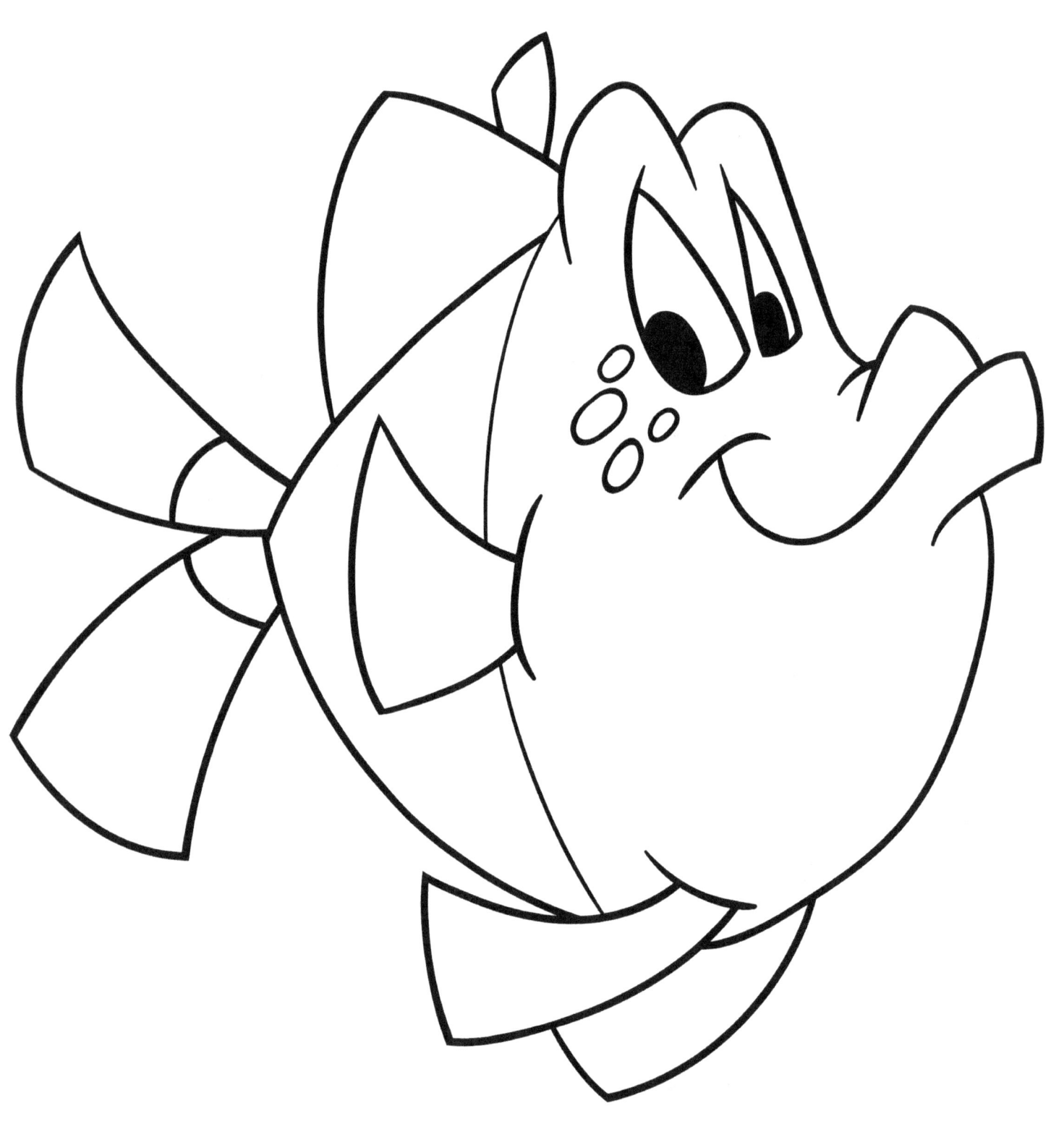

FIND THE DIFFERENT PICTURE

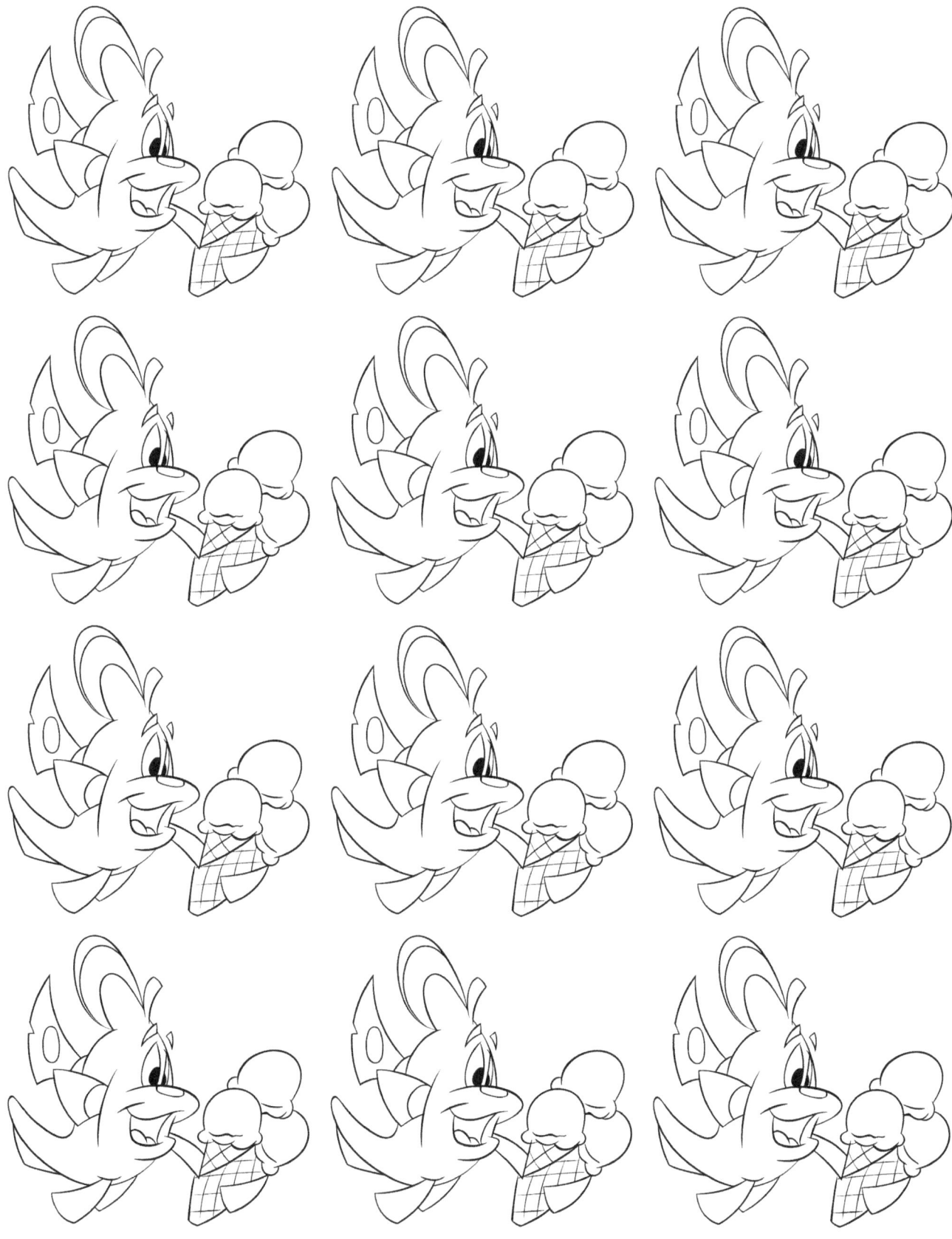

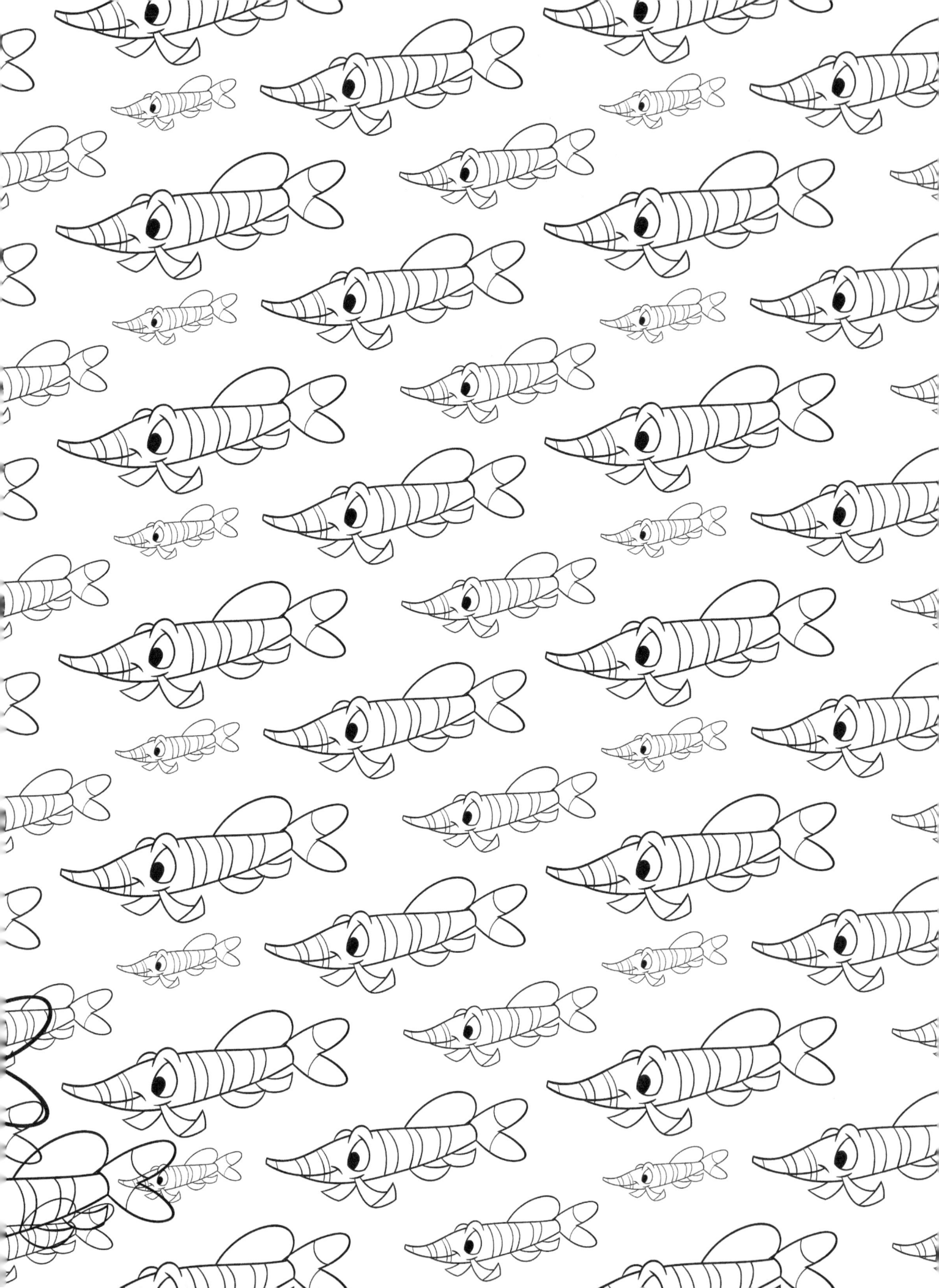

SQUARES

TAKE TURNS, CONNECT A LINE FROM ONE PLANKTON TO ANOTHER. WHOEVER MAKES THE LINE THAT COMPLETES THE BOX PUTS THEIR INITALS INSID THAT BOX. THE PERSON WITH THE MOST SQUARES AT THE END OF THE GAME WINS!

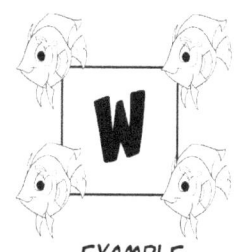

EXAMPLE

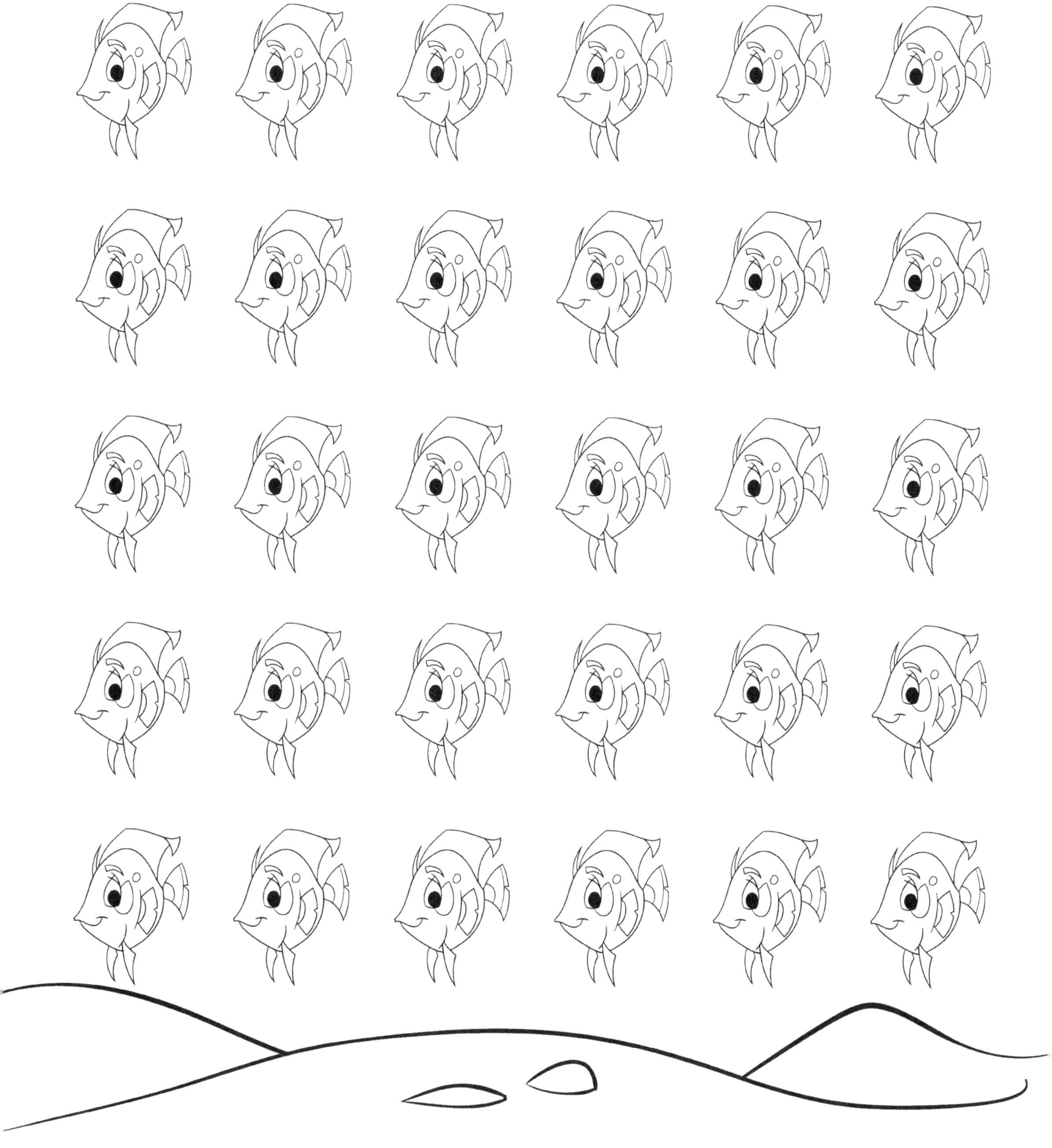

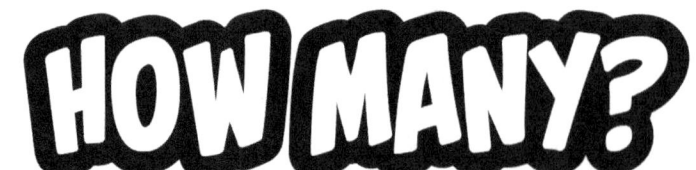

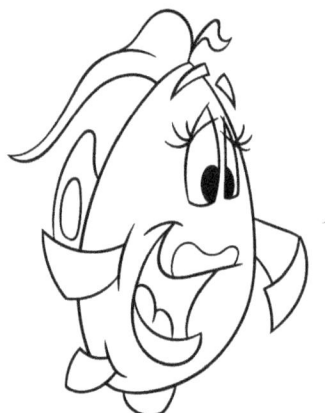

HOW MANY WORDS CAN YOU MAKE USING THE LETTERS BELOW.

MEGAMOUTH SHARK

EXAMPLE: **ART**

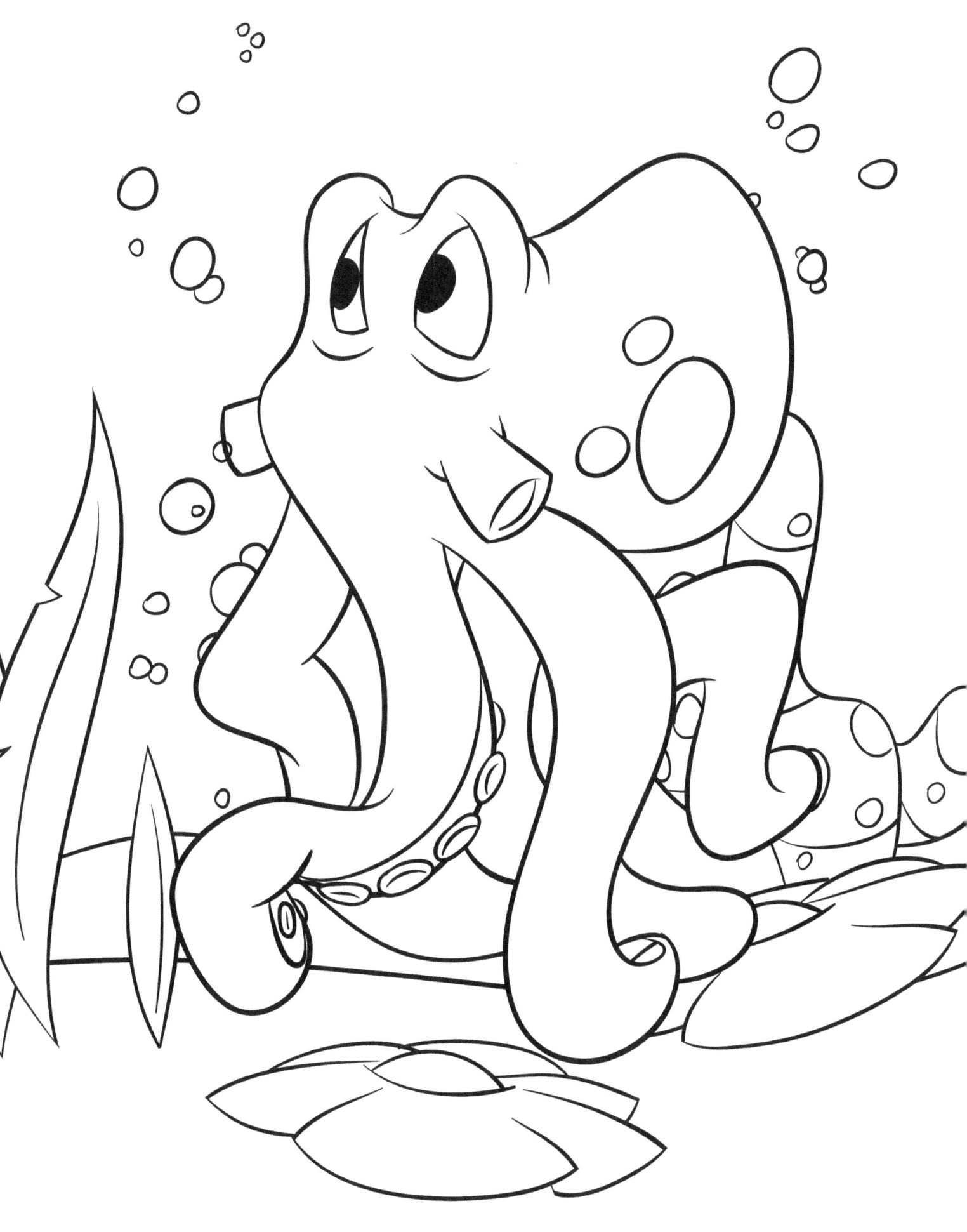

WORD SCRAMBLE

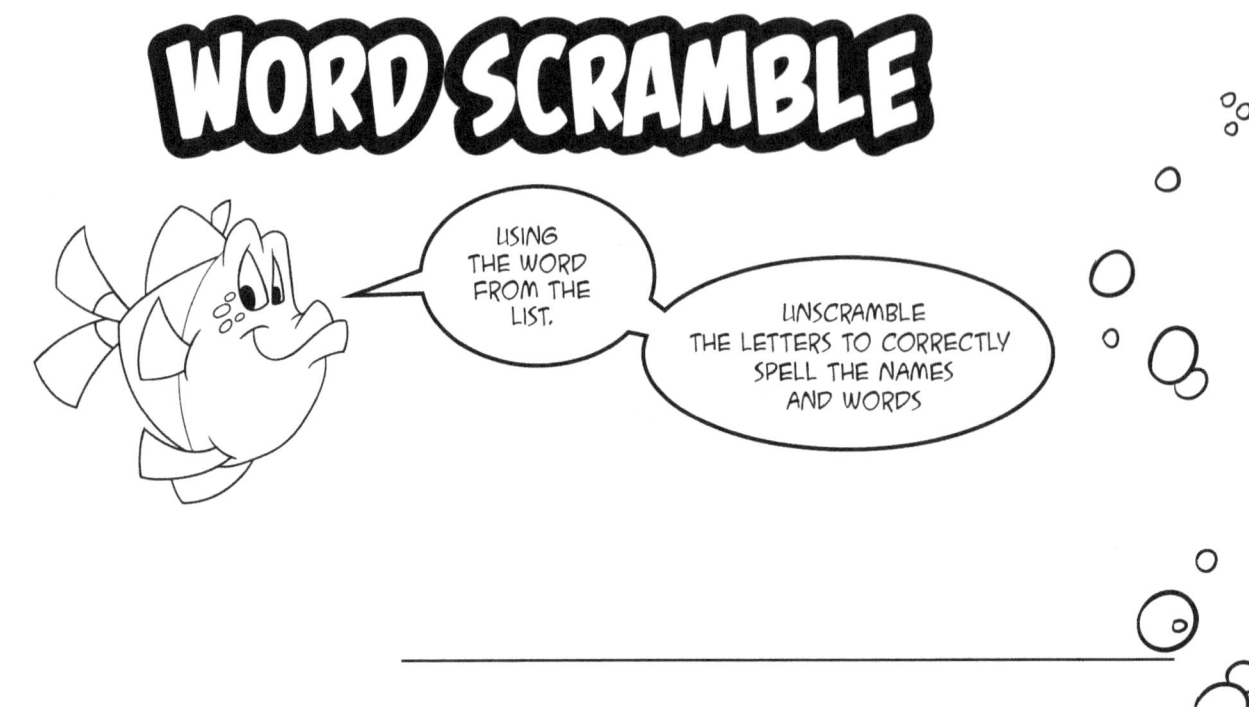

LAIS _____

NELOYCC _____

MHYLPU _____

ERFE _____

KHRAS _____

DNAS _____

REASHOSE _____

DSASIEE _____

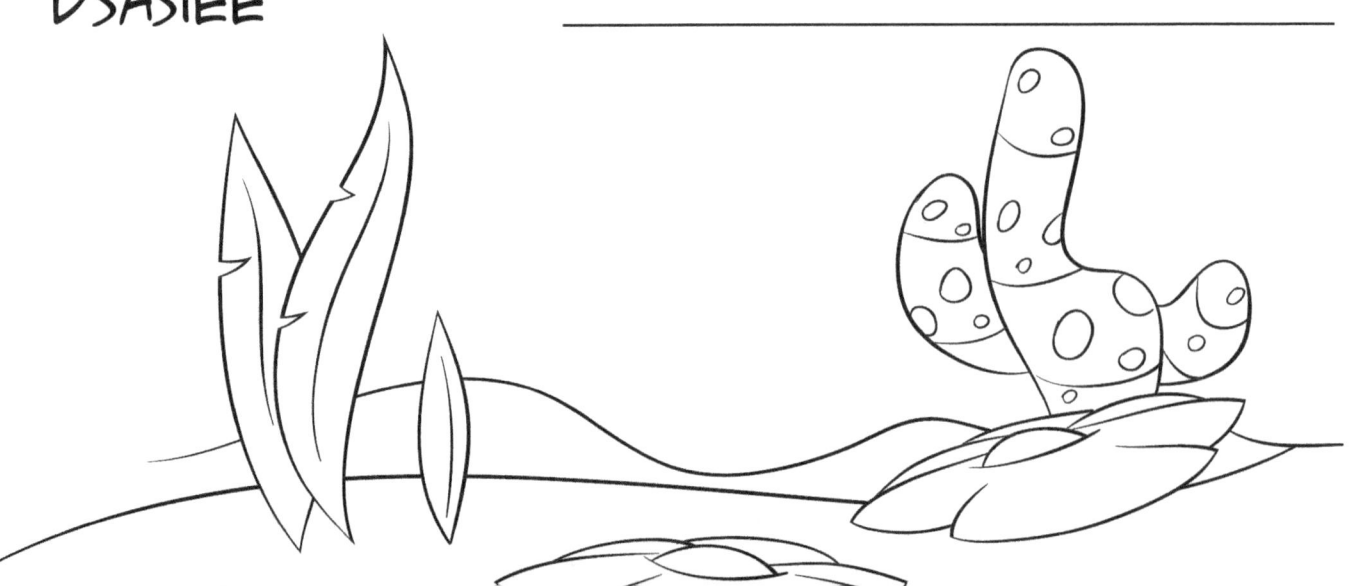

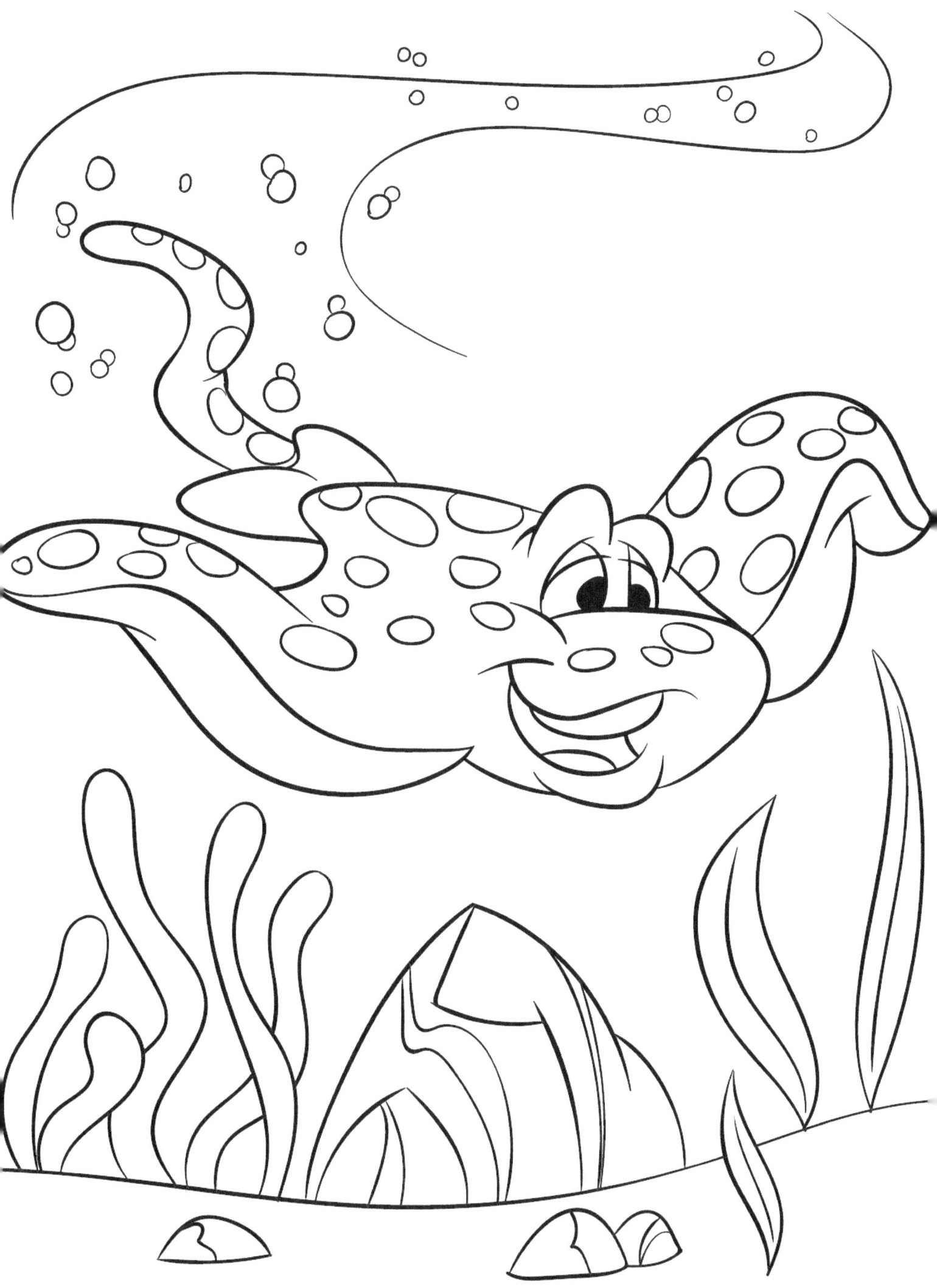

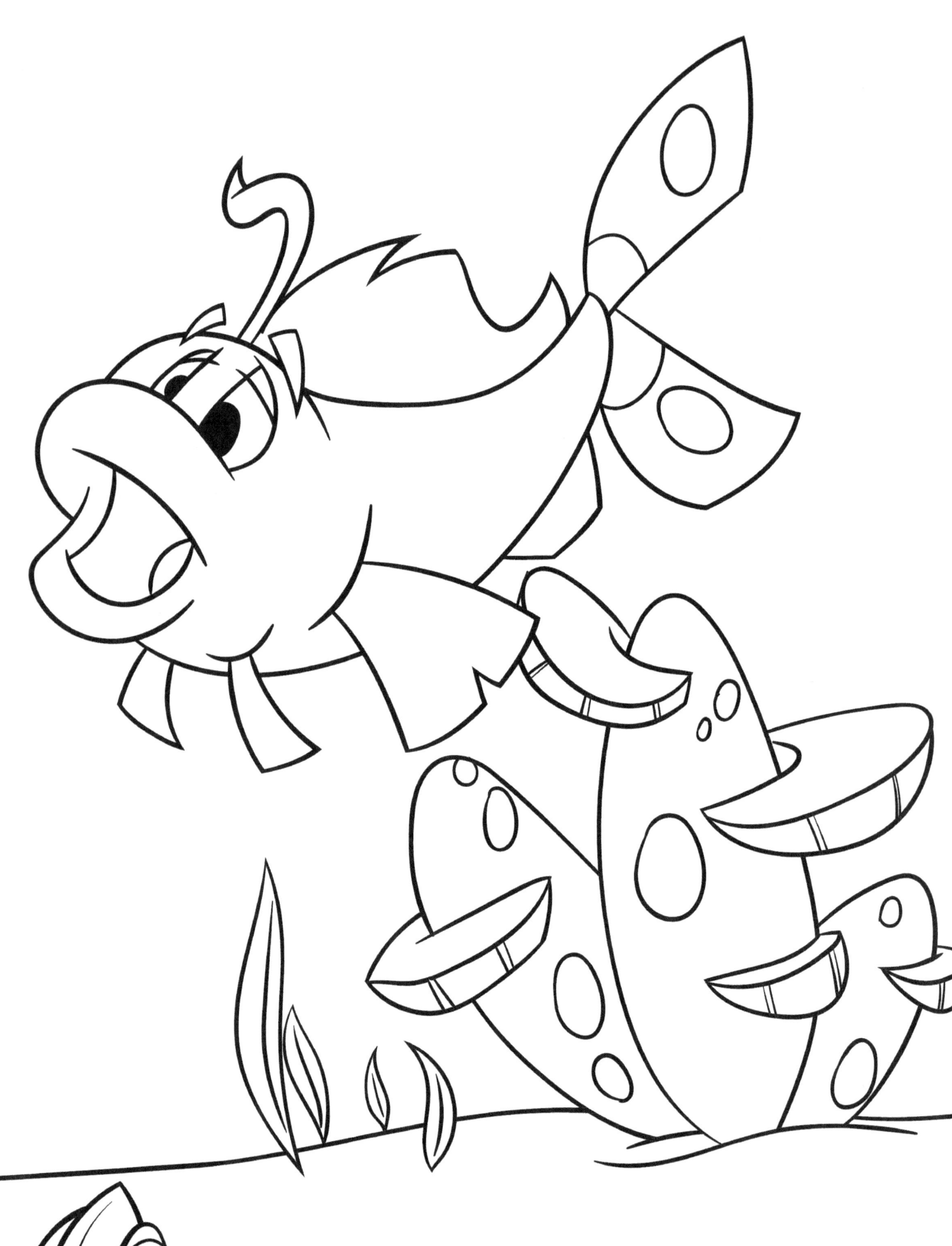

Find the Different Shadow

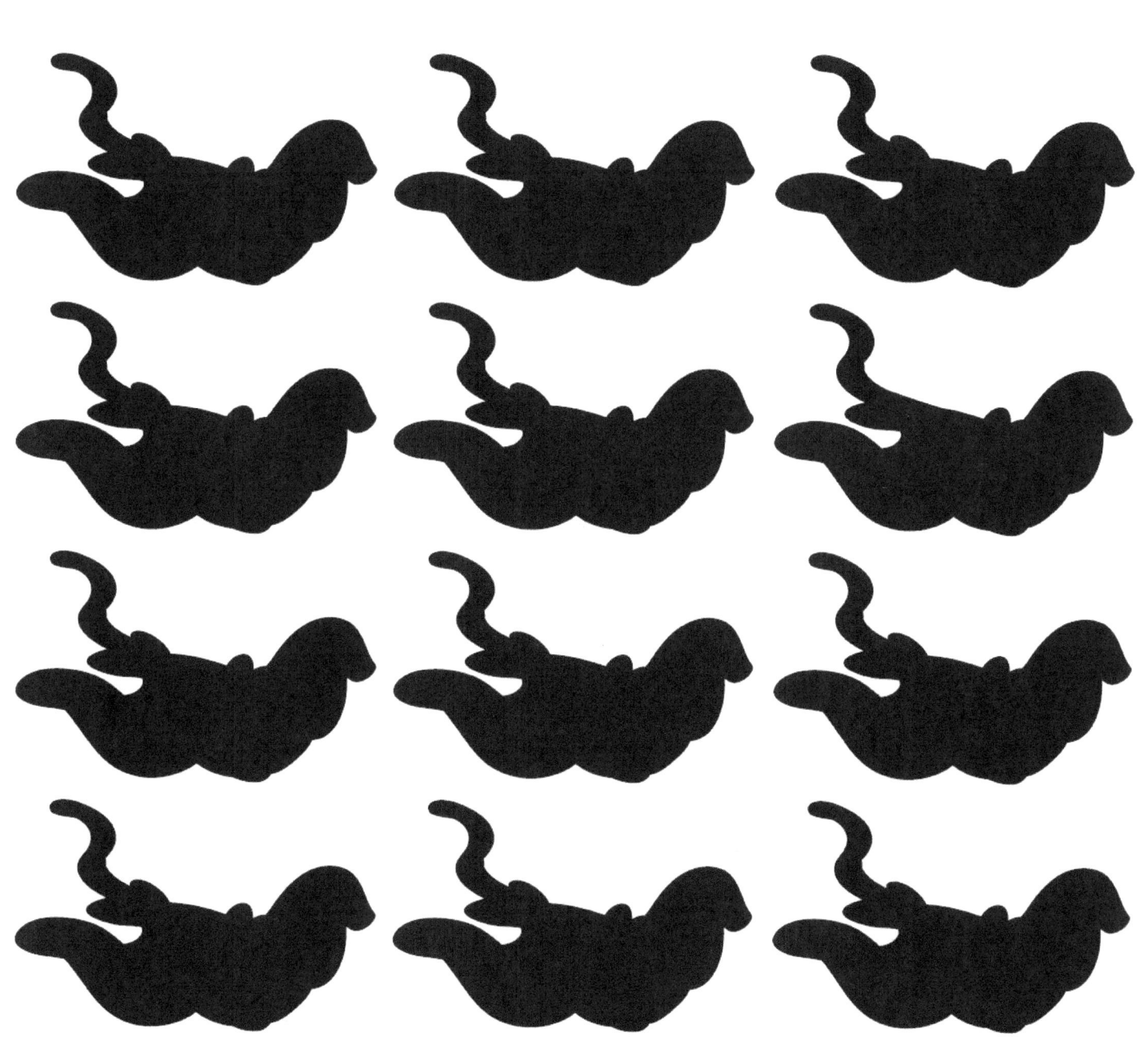

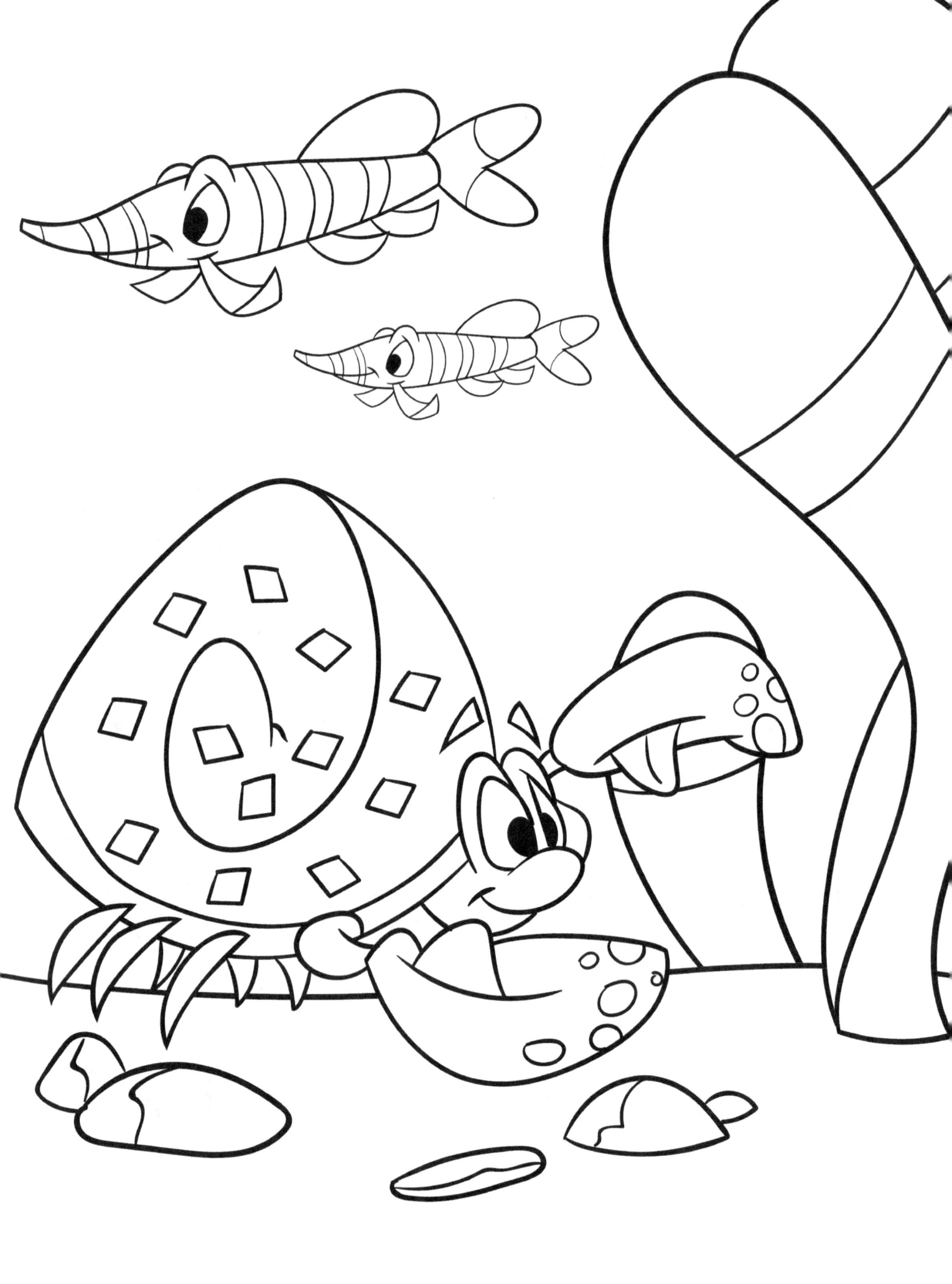

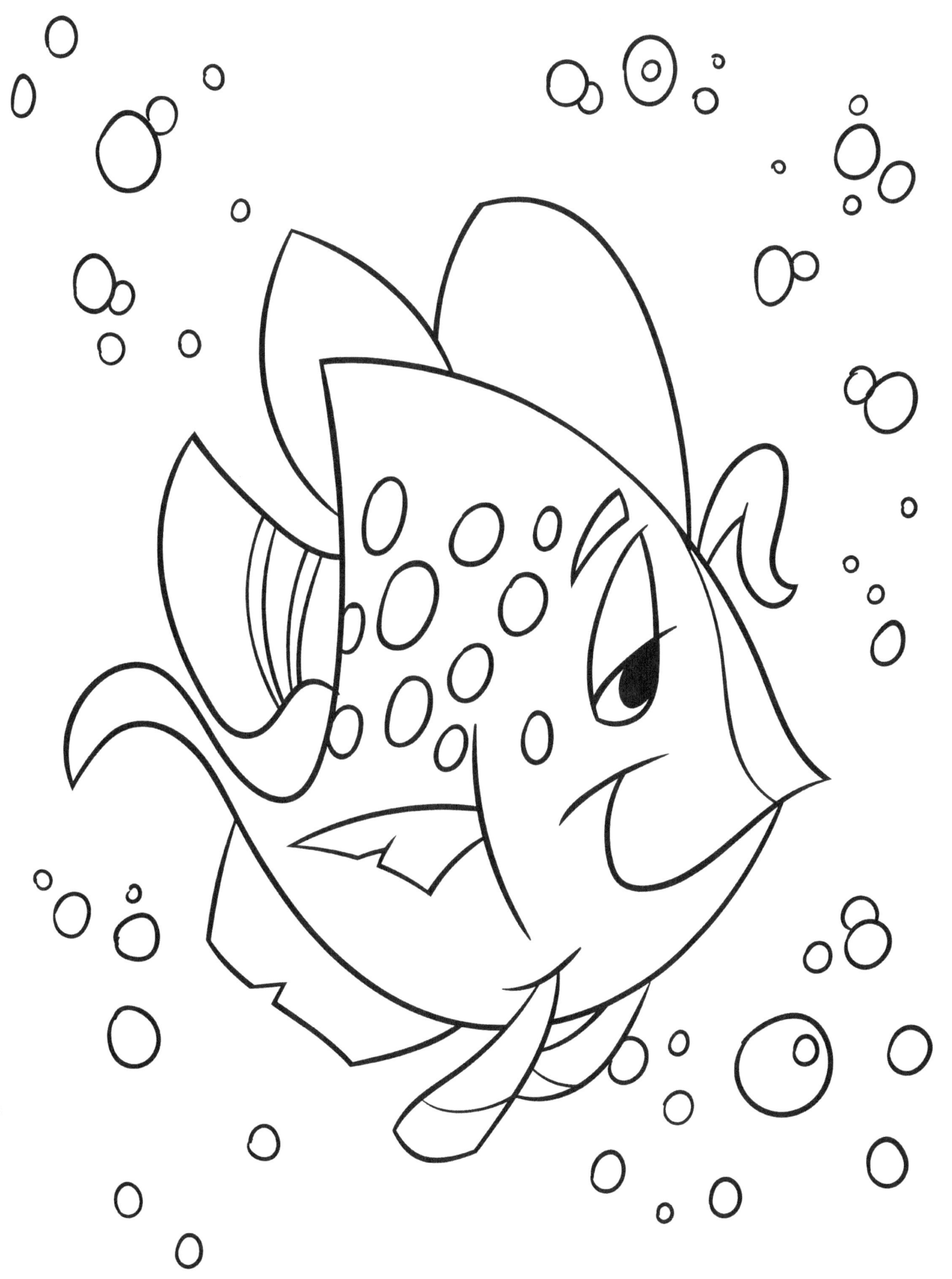

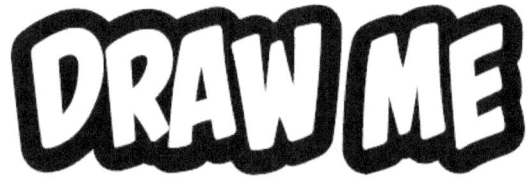

USE THE GRID TO HELP
YOU DRAW THIS FISH.

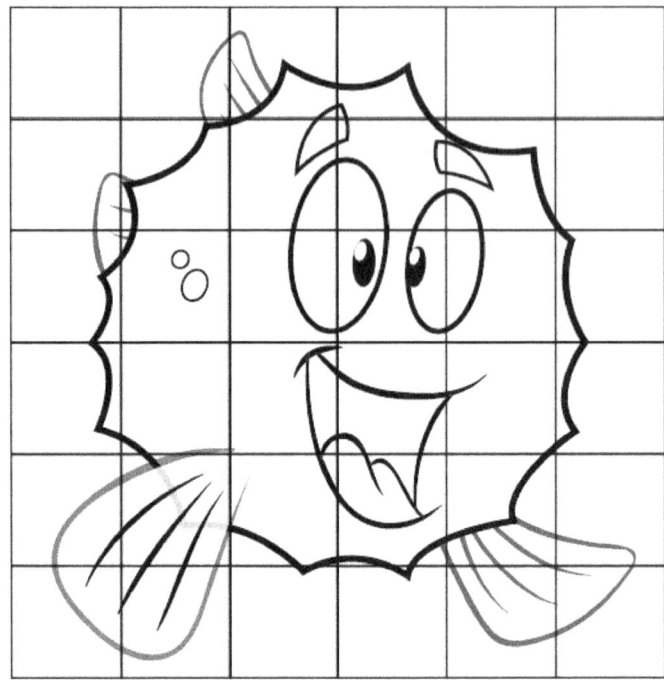

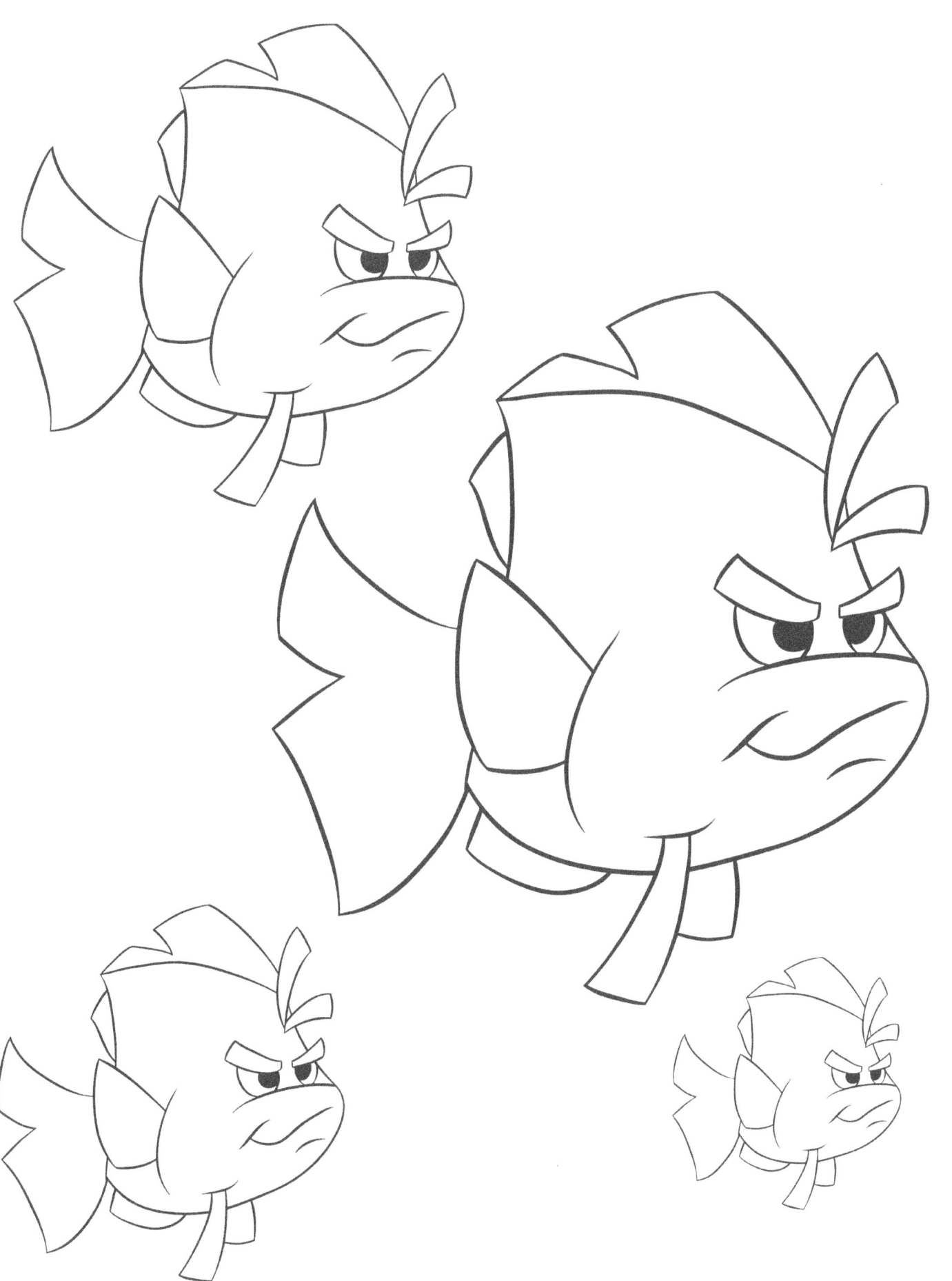

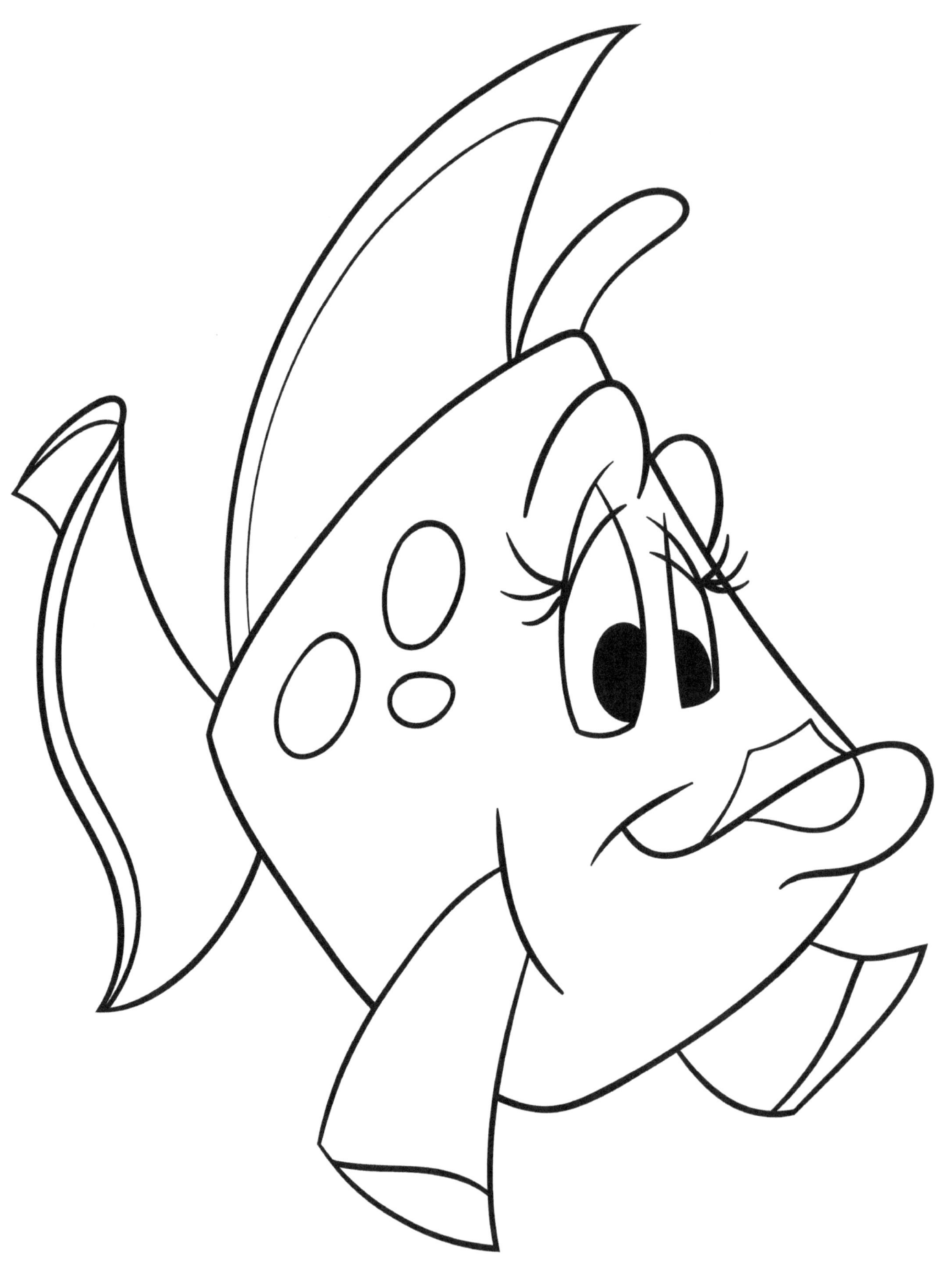

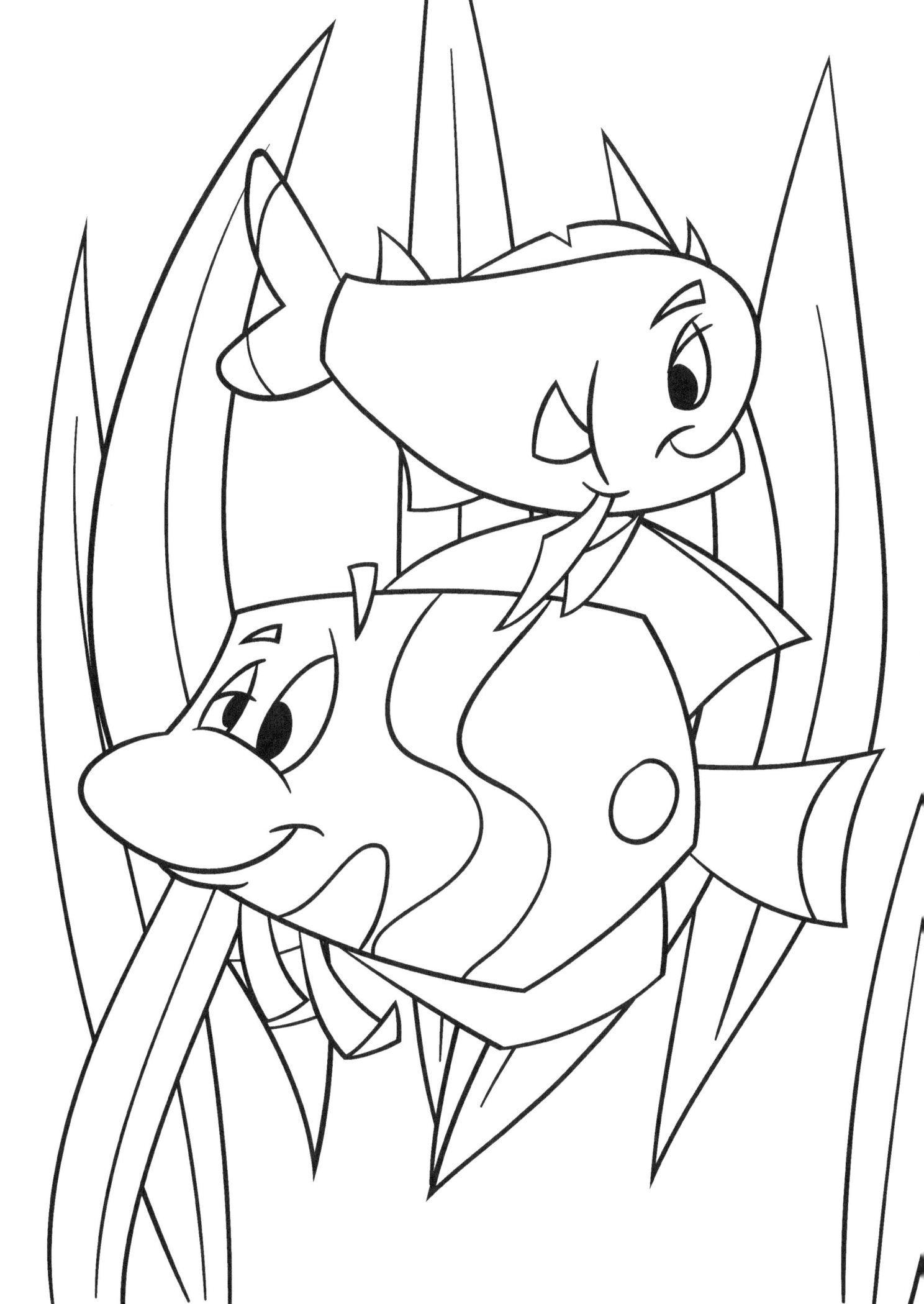

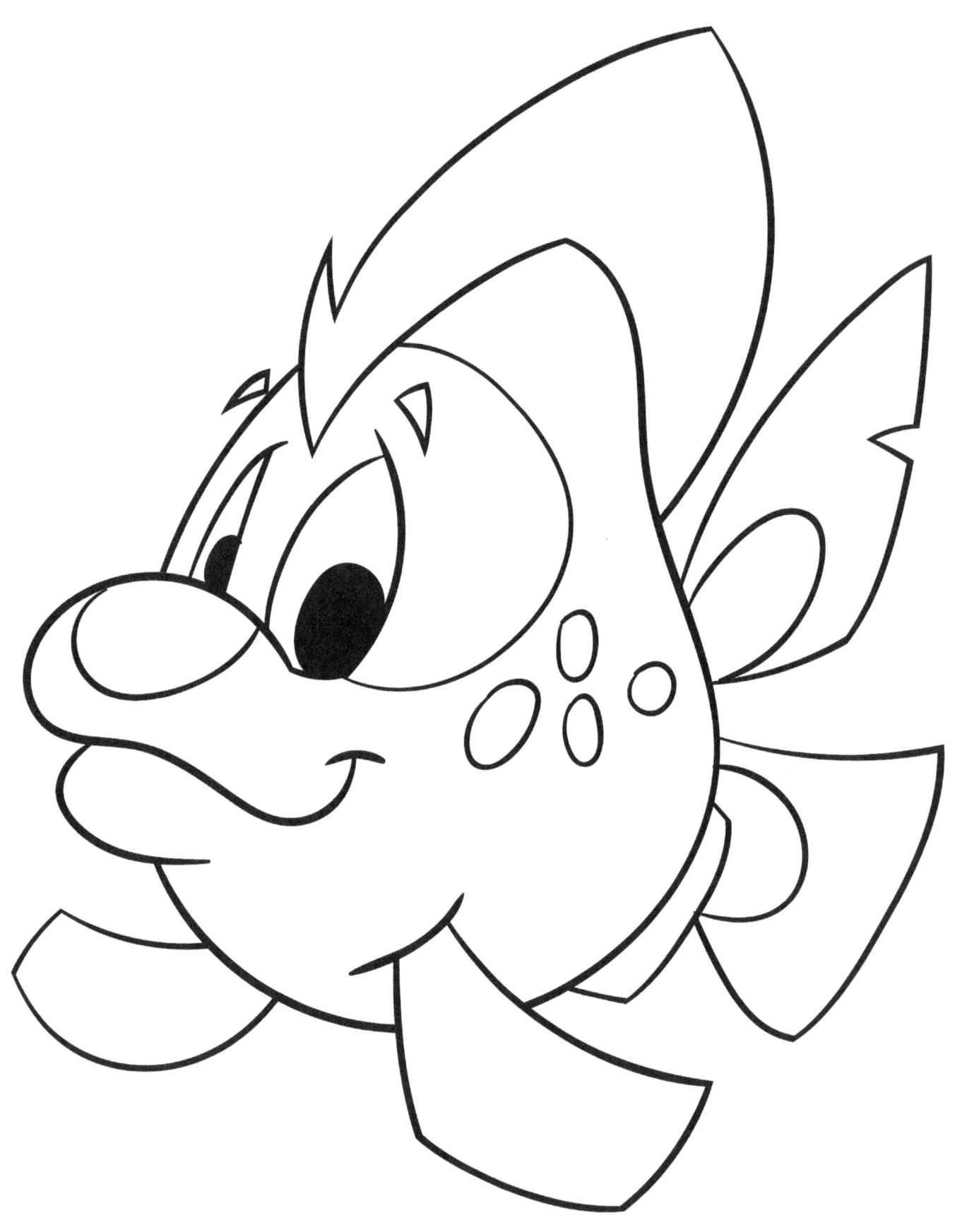

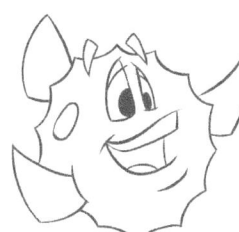 # FIND YOUR WAY OUT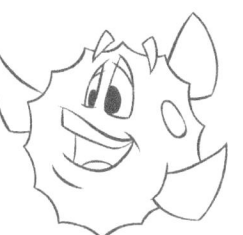

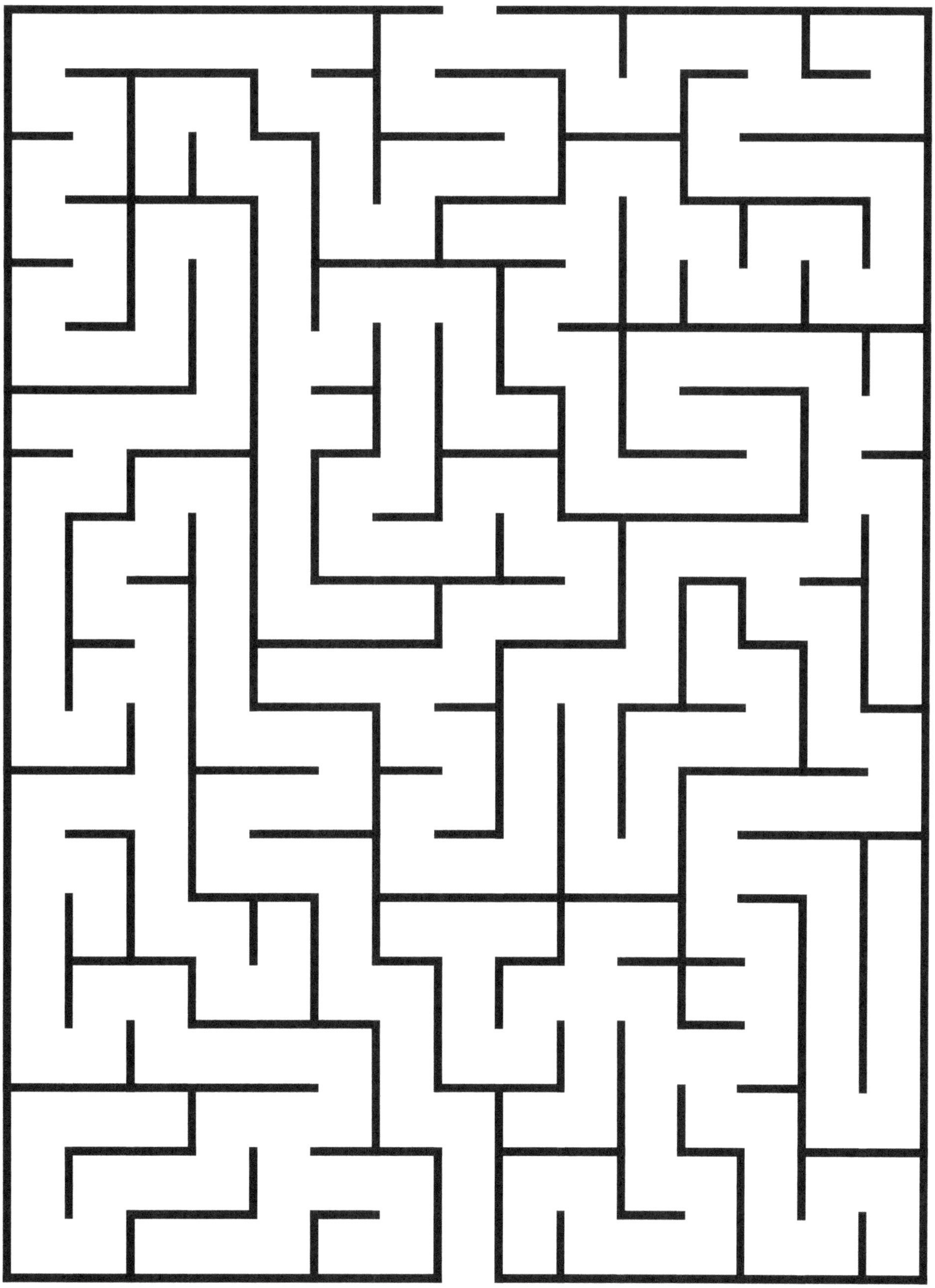

WORD SCRAMBLE

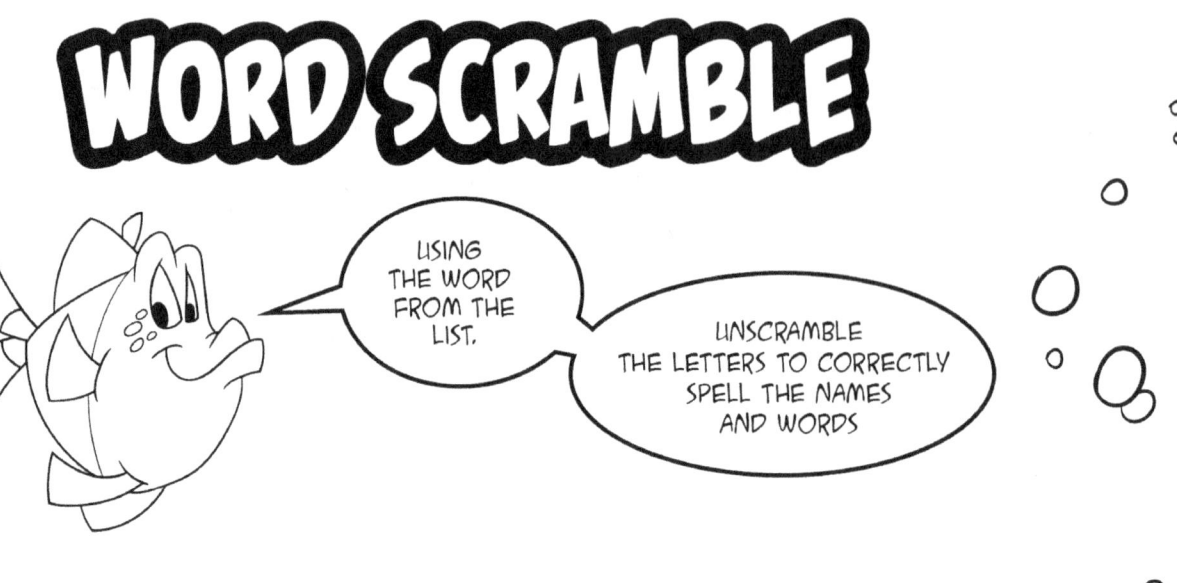

IANR _____

HSISP _____

EMIANR _____

DISNSAL _____

RABORH _____

CAEBH _____

GOLANO _____

ACOTS _____

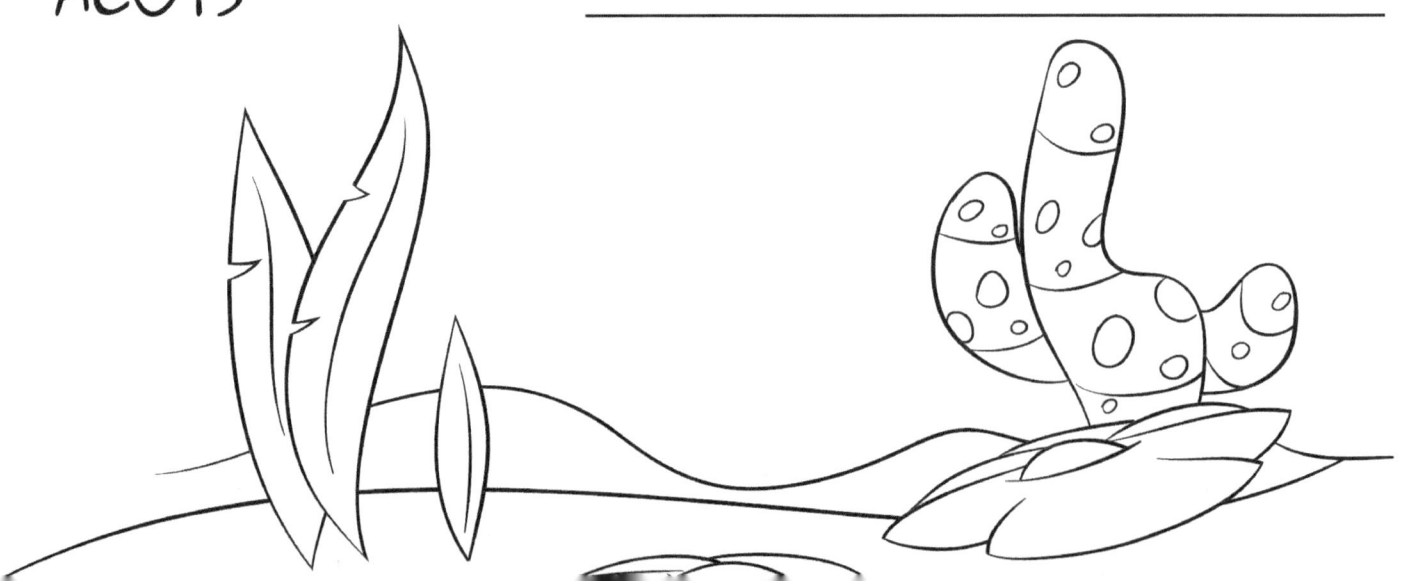

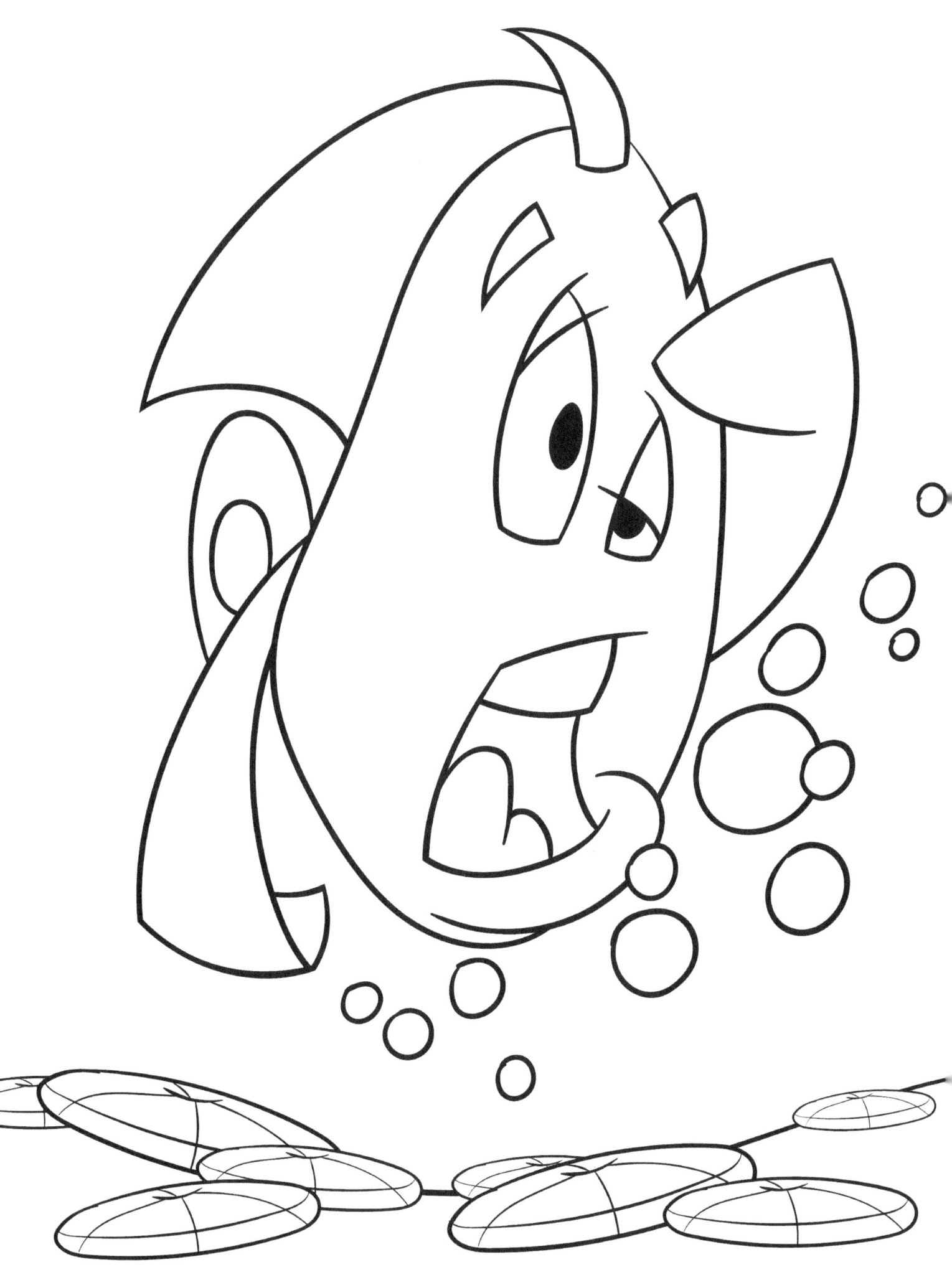

FIND THE DIFFERENT PICTURE

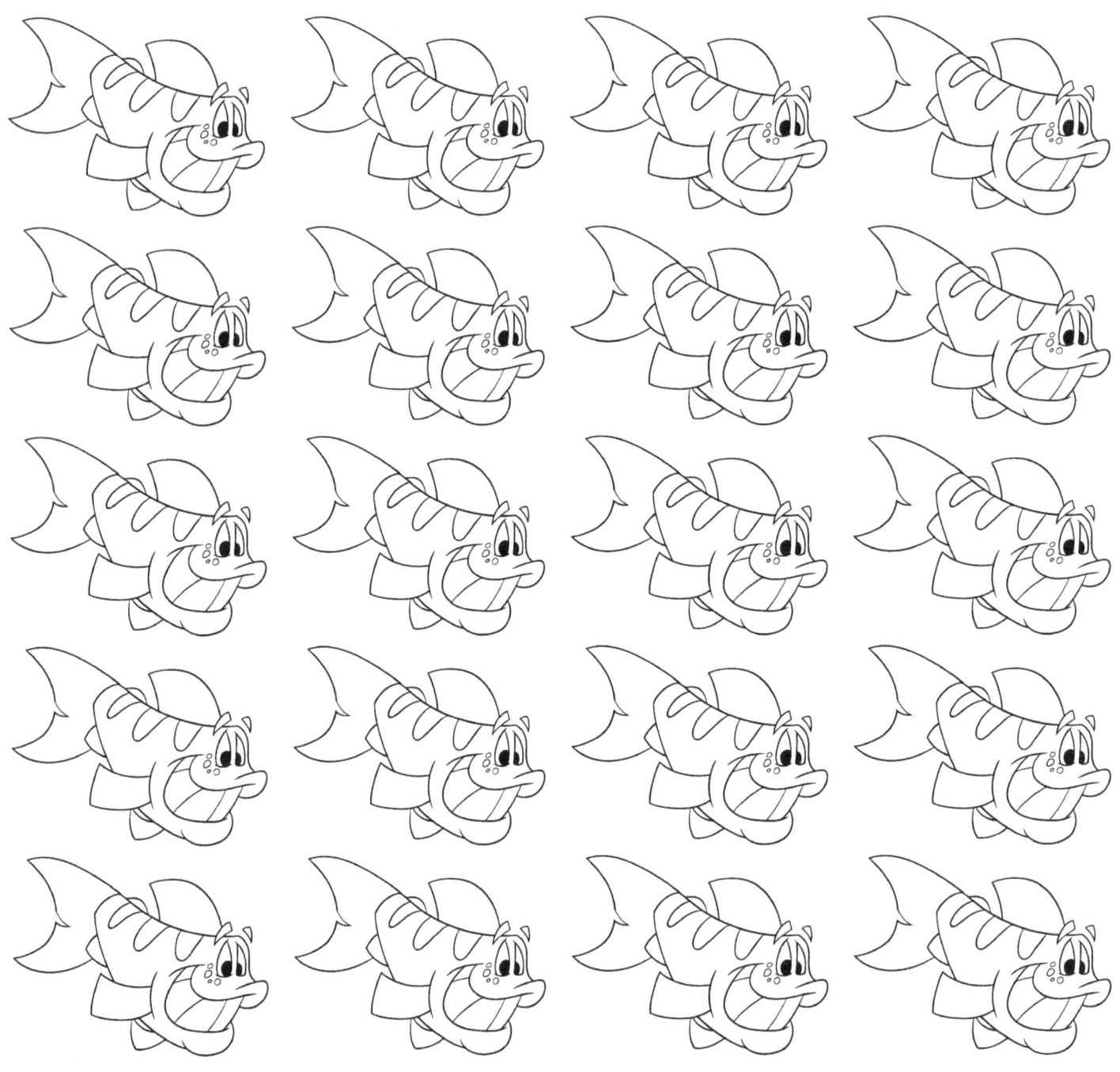

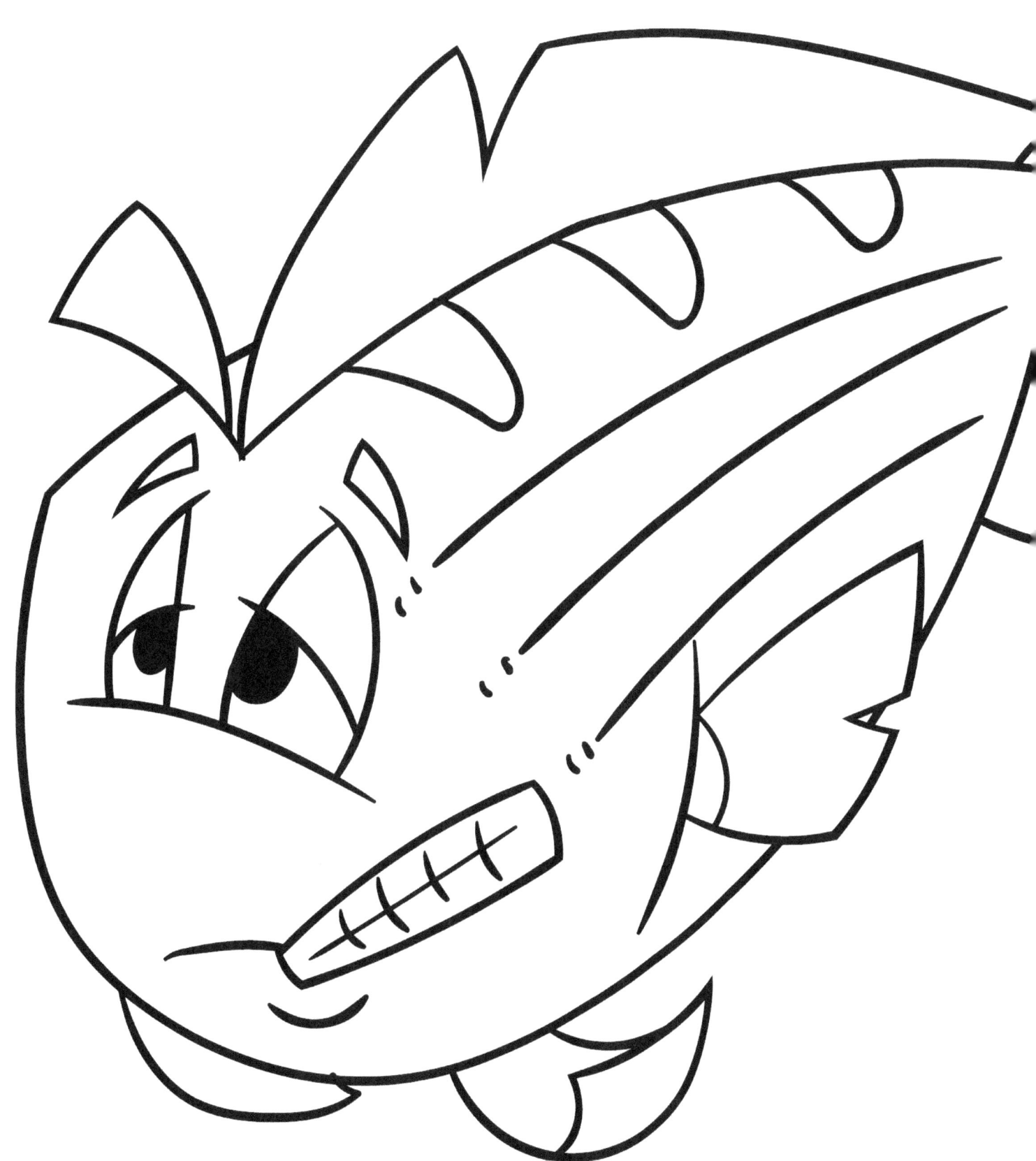

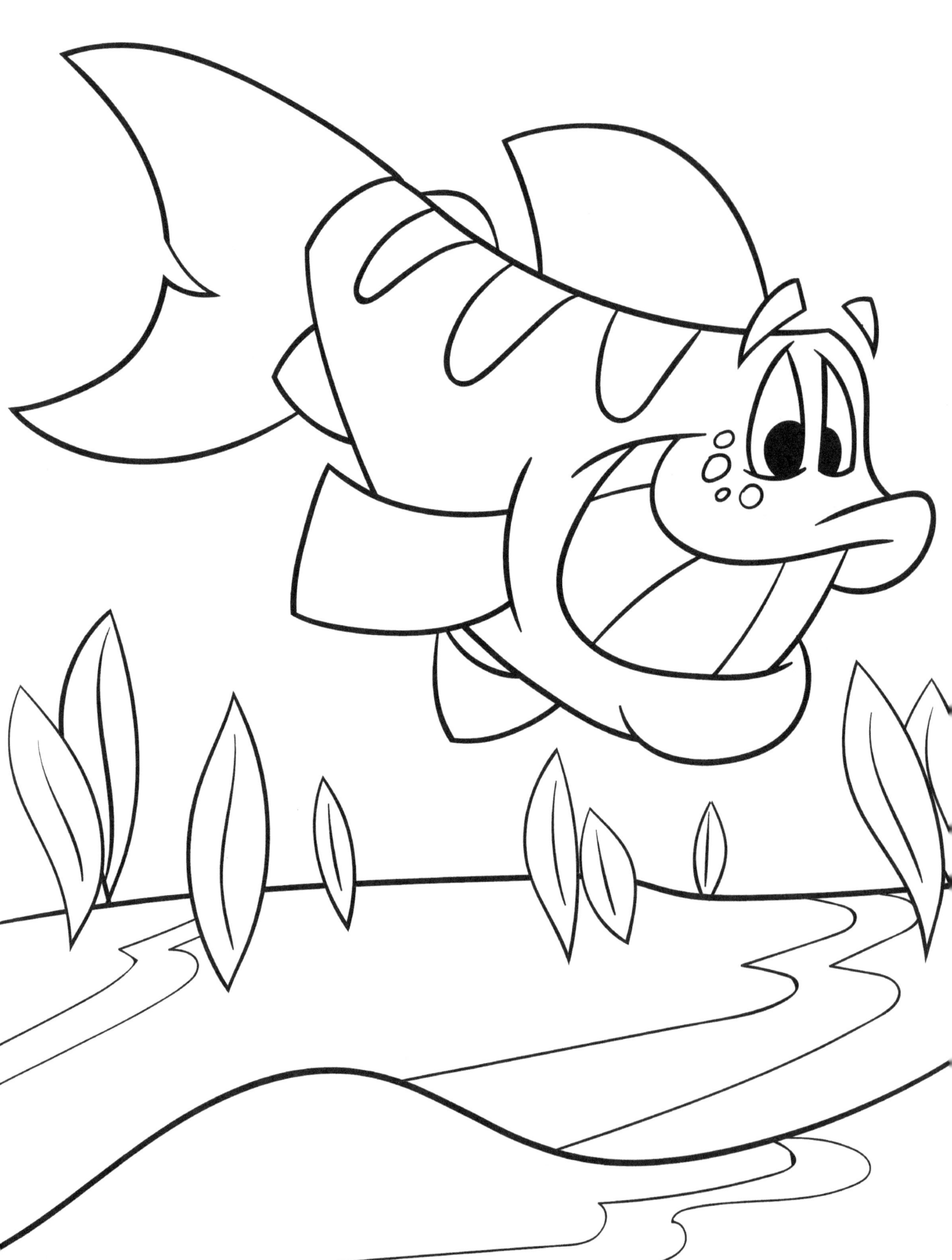

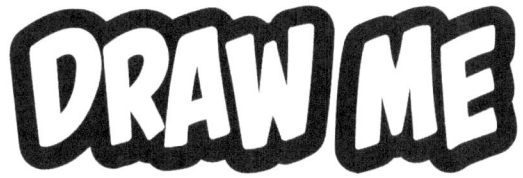

USE THE GRID TO HELP
YOU DRAW THIS FISH.

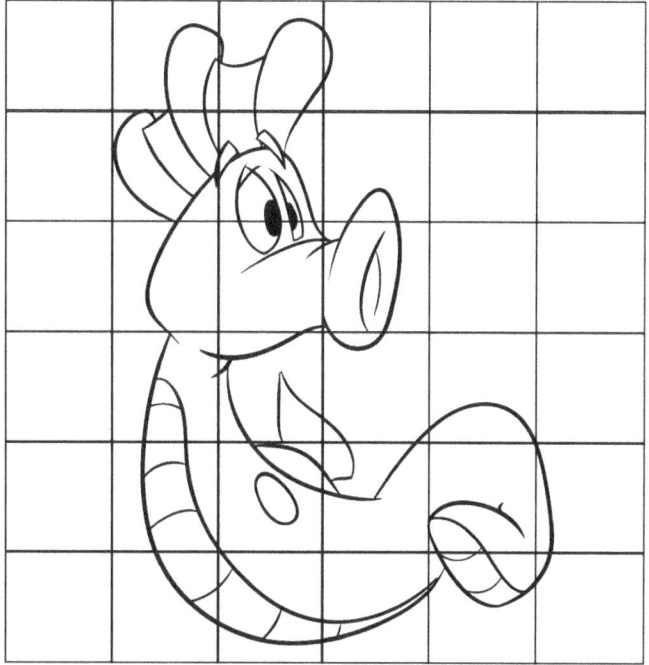

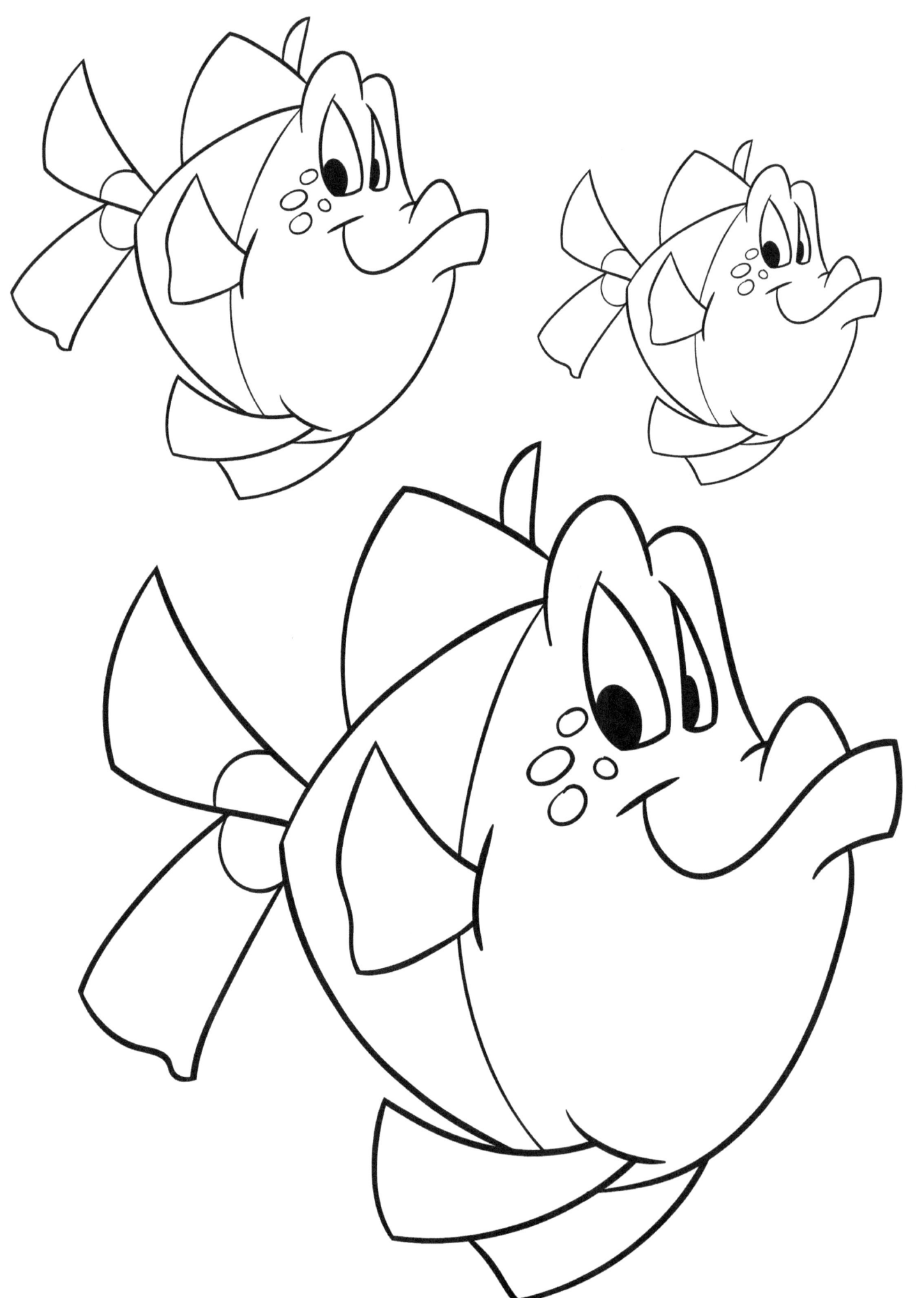

Find the Different Shadow

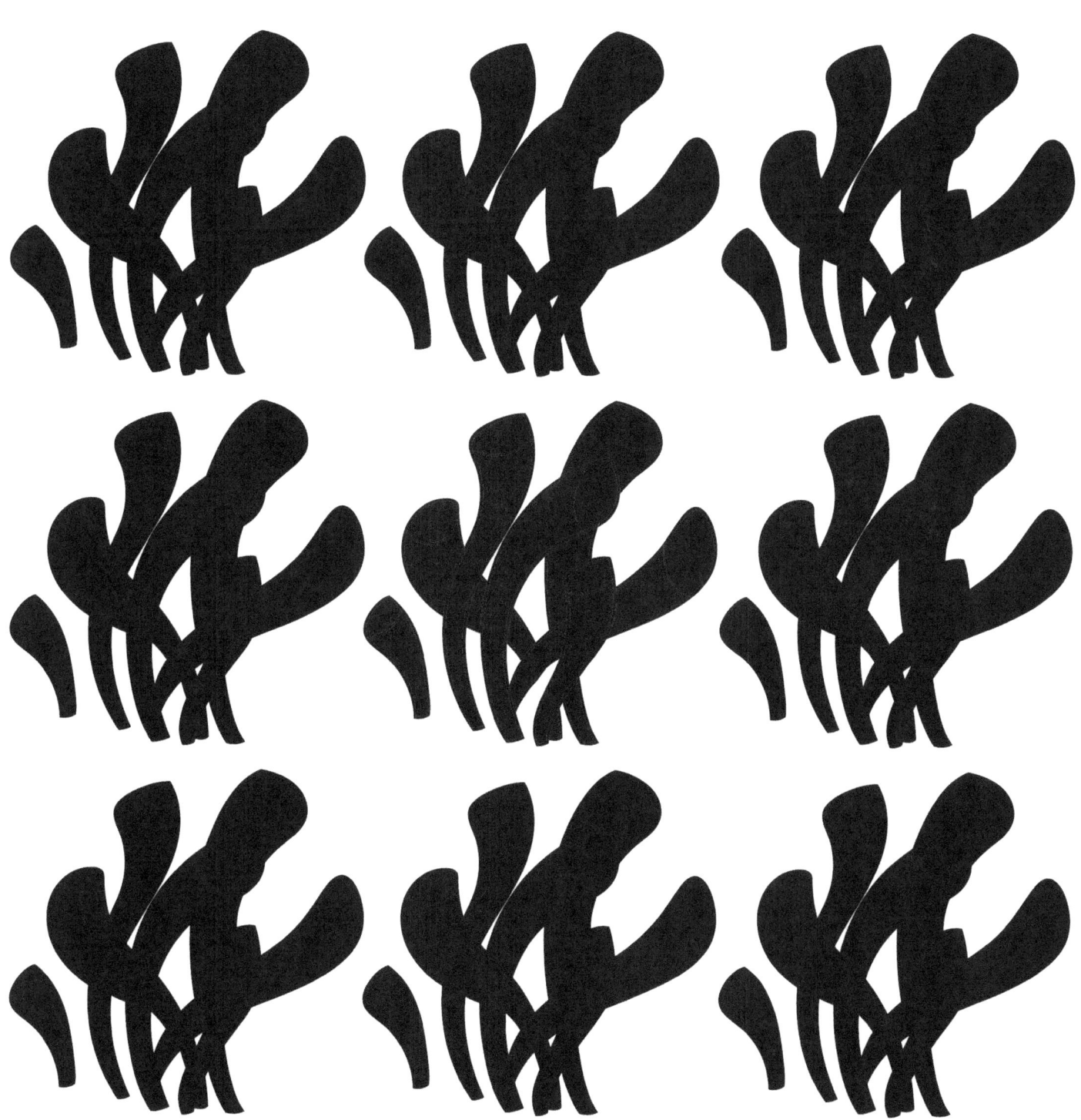

Find the Different Picture

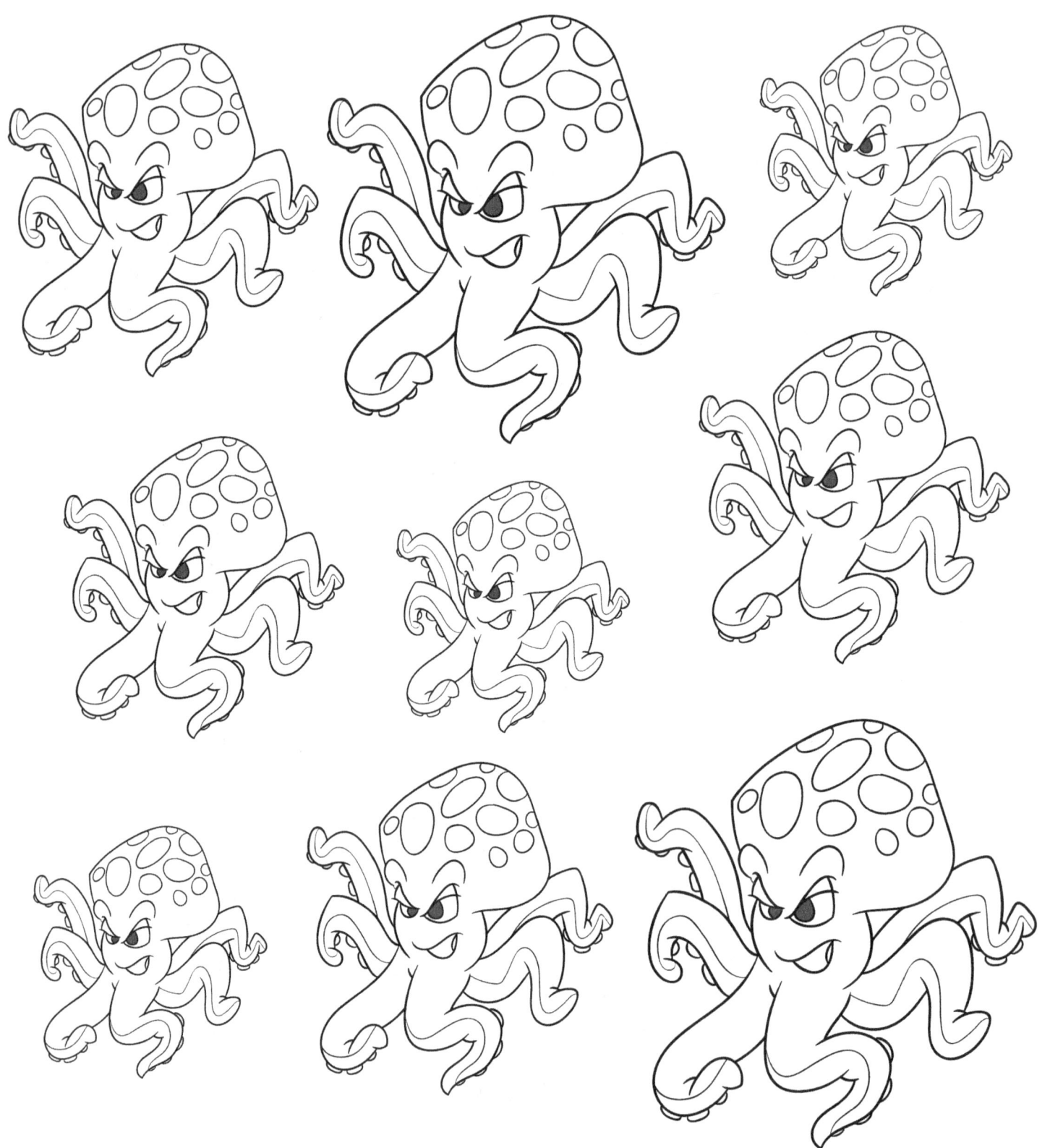

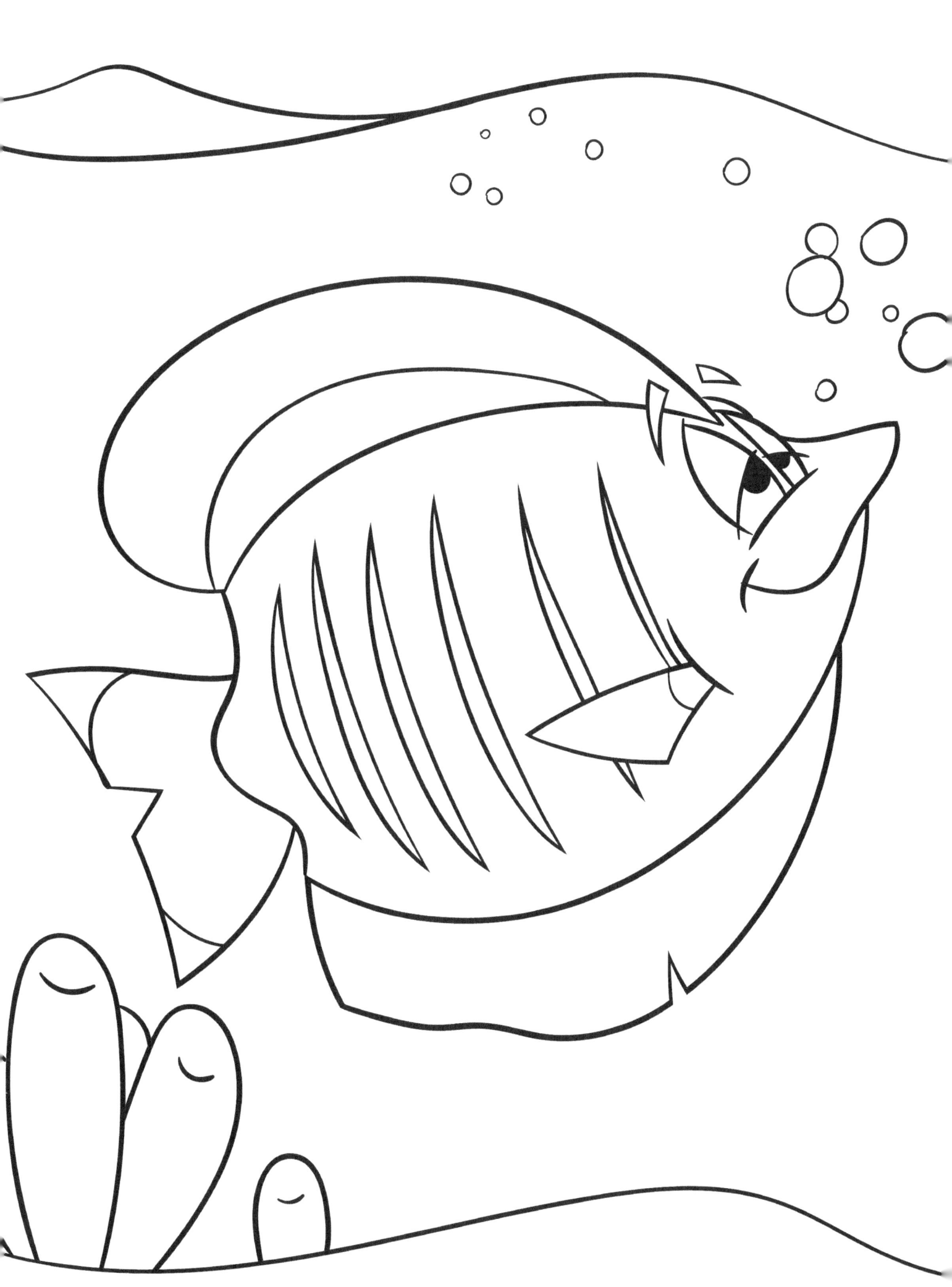

SQUARES

TAKE TURNS, CONNECT A LINE FROM ONE PLANKTON TO ANOTHER. WHOEVER MAKES THE LINE THAT COMPLETES THE BOX PUTS THEIR INITALS INSID THAT BOX. THE PERSON WITH THE MOST SQUARES AT THE END OF THE GAME WINS!

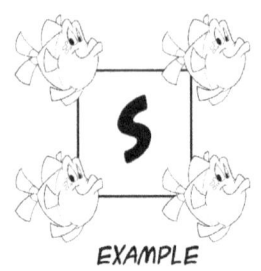

EXAMPLE

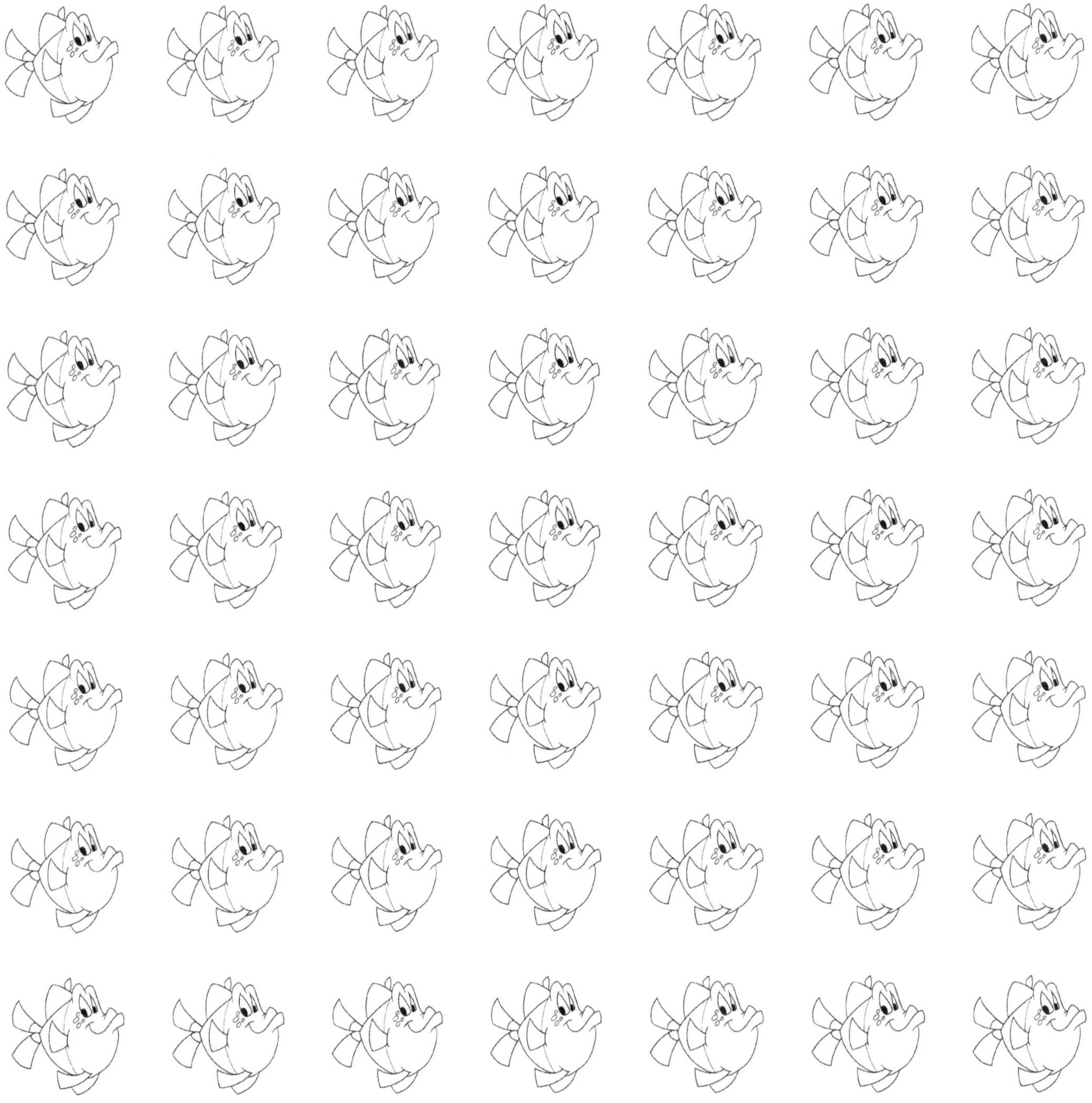

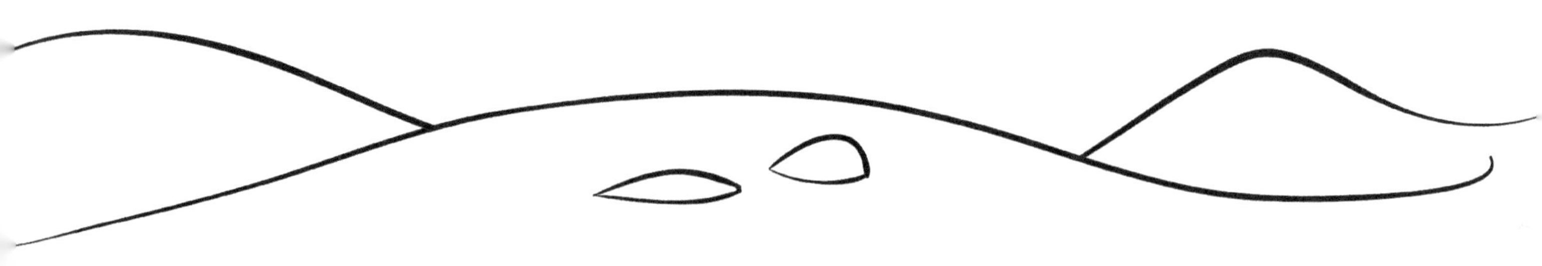

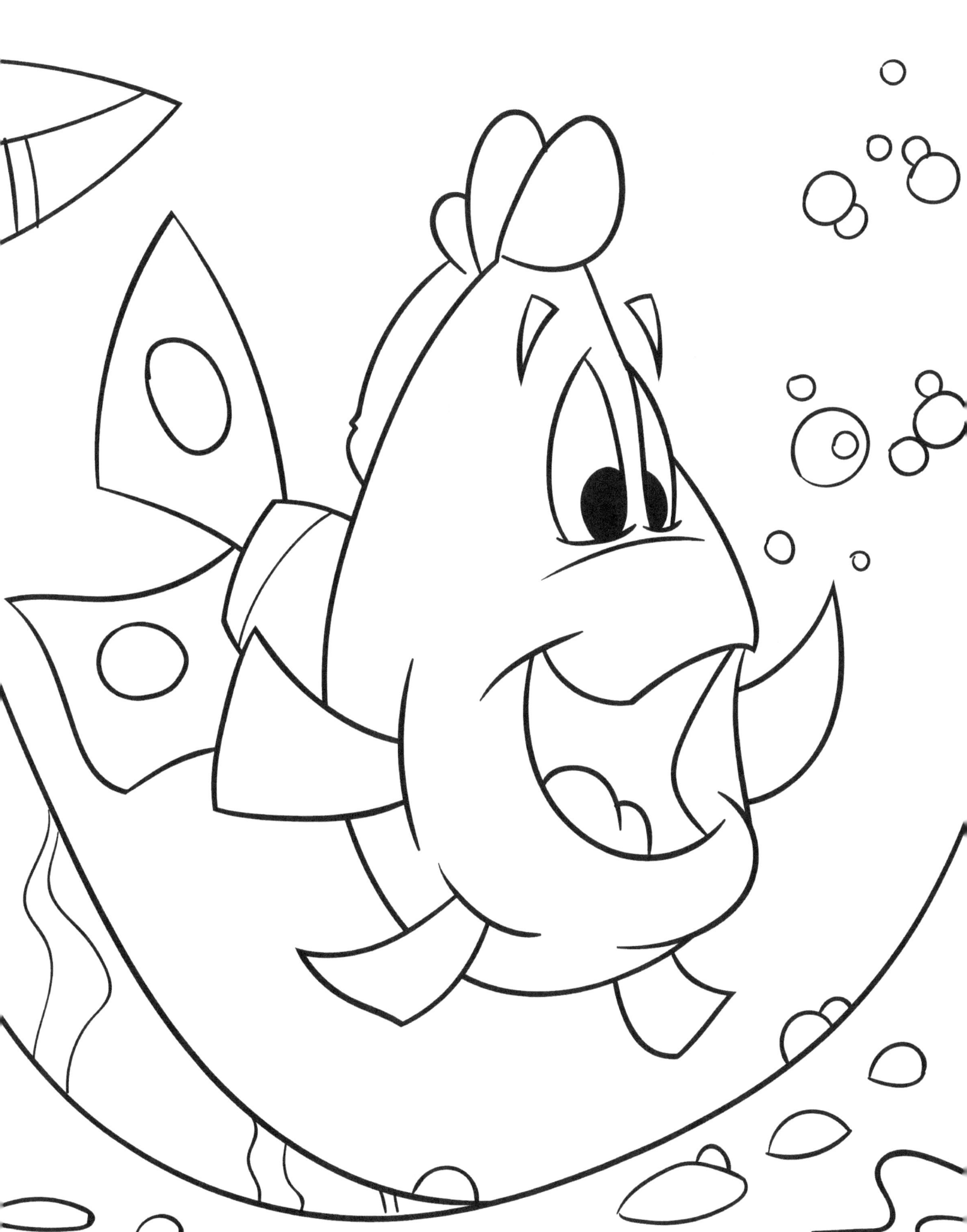

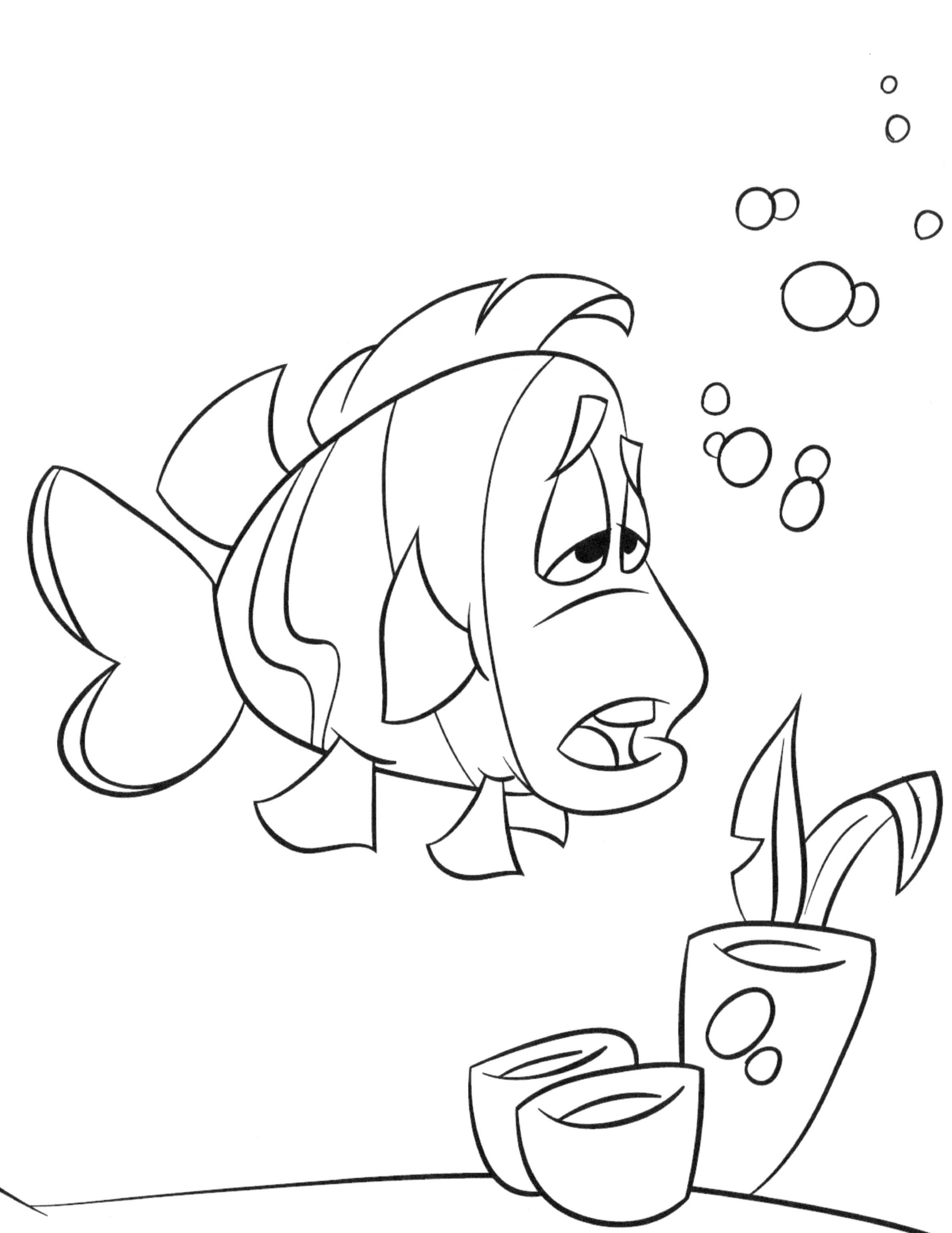

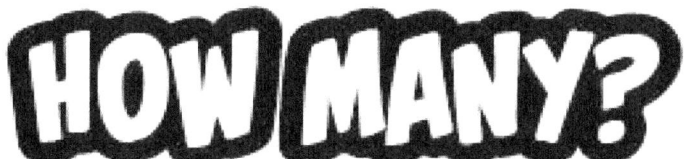

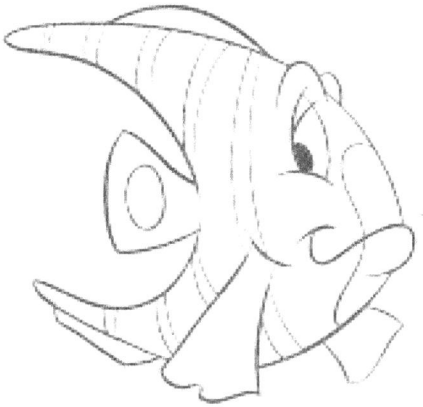

HOW MANY WORDS CAN YOU MAKE USING THE LETTERS BELOW.

BIOLOGICAL FILTRATION

EXAMPLE: FOOT

FIND THE DIFFERENT PICTURE

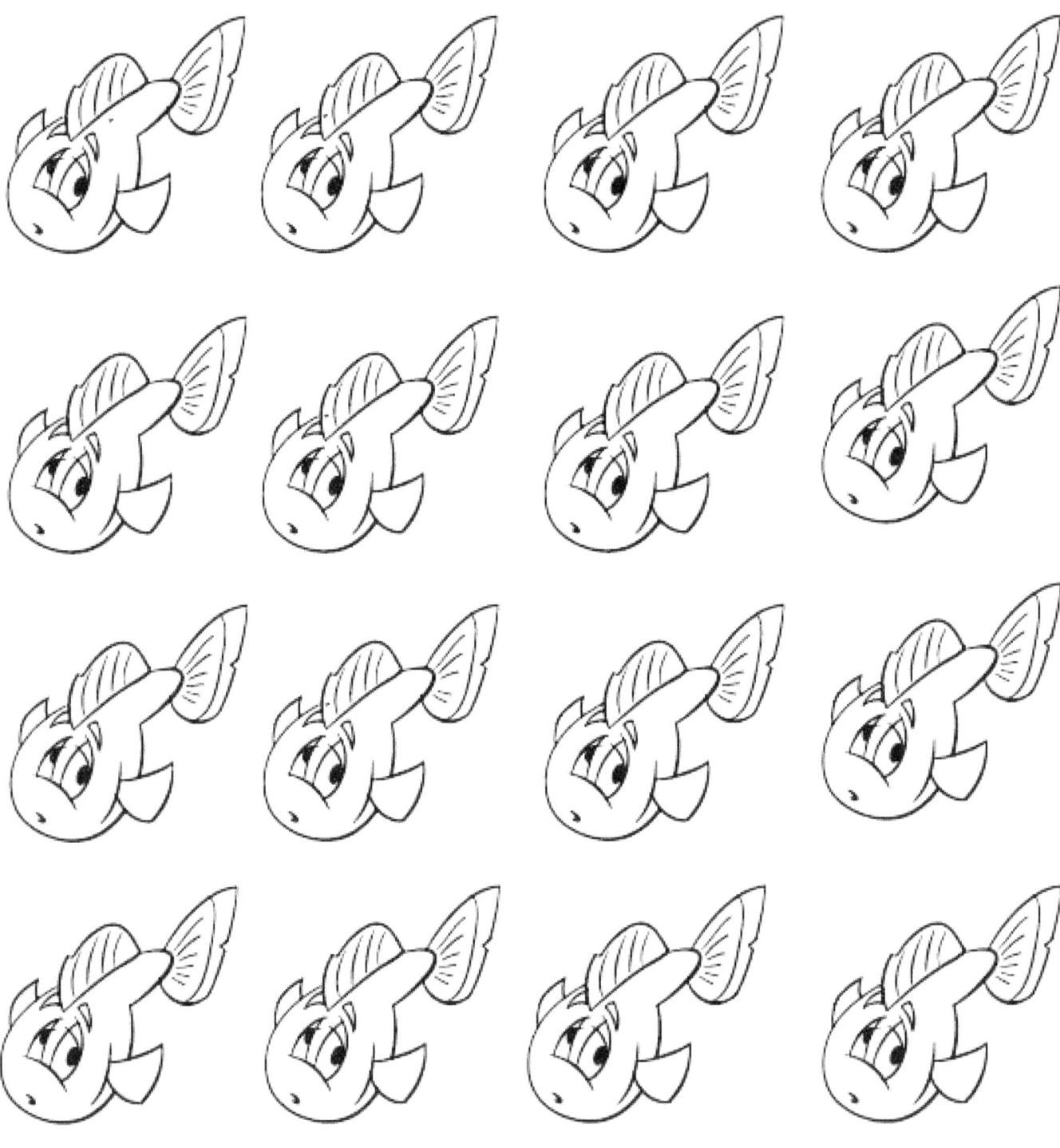

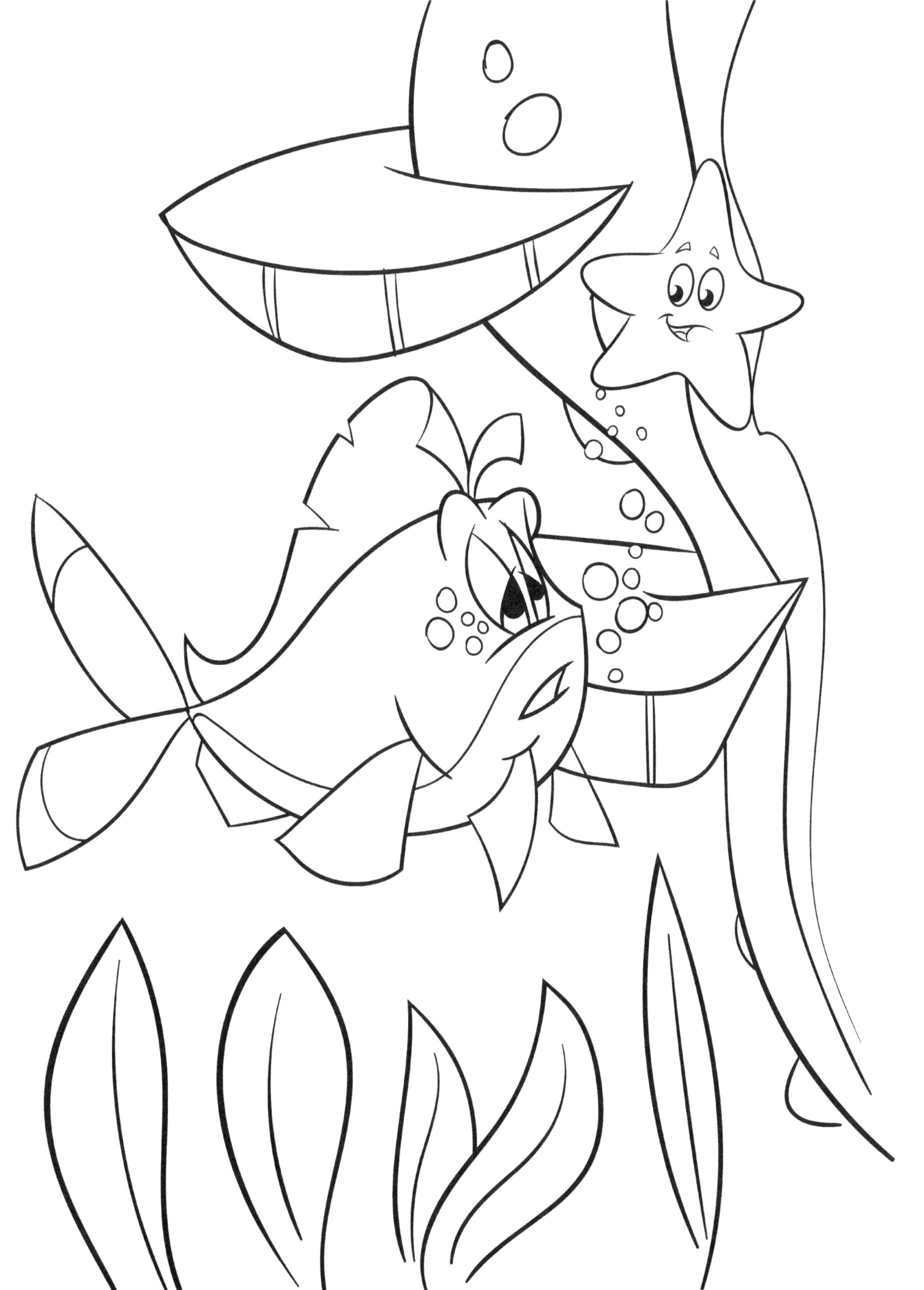

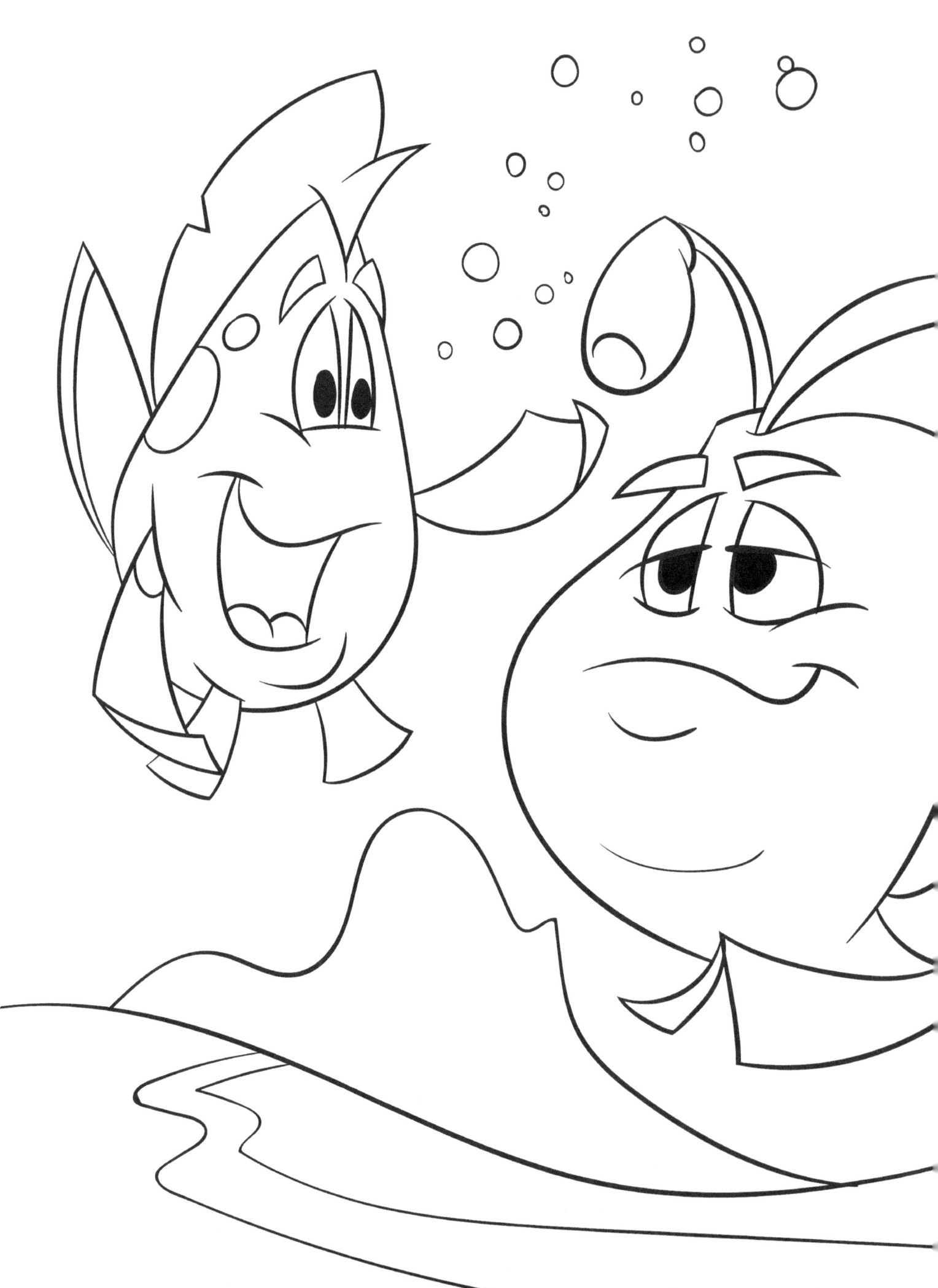

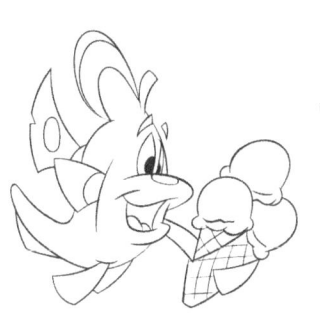
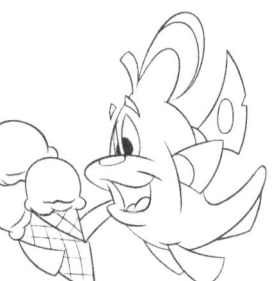

FIND YOUR WAY OUT

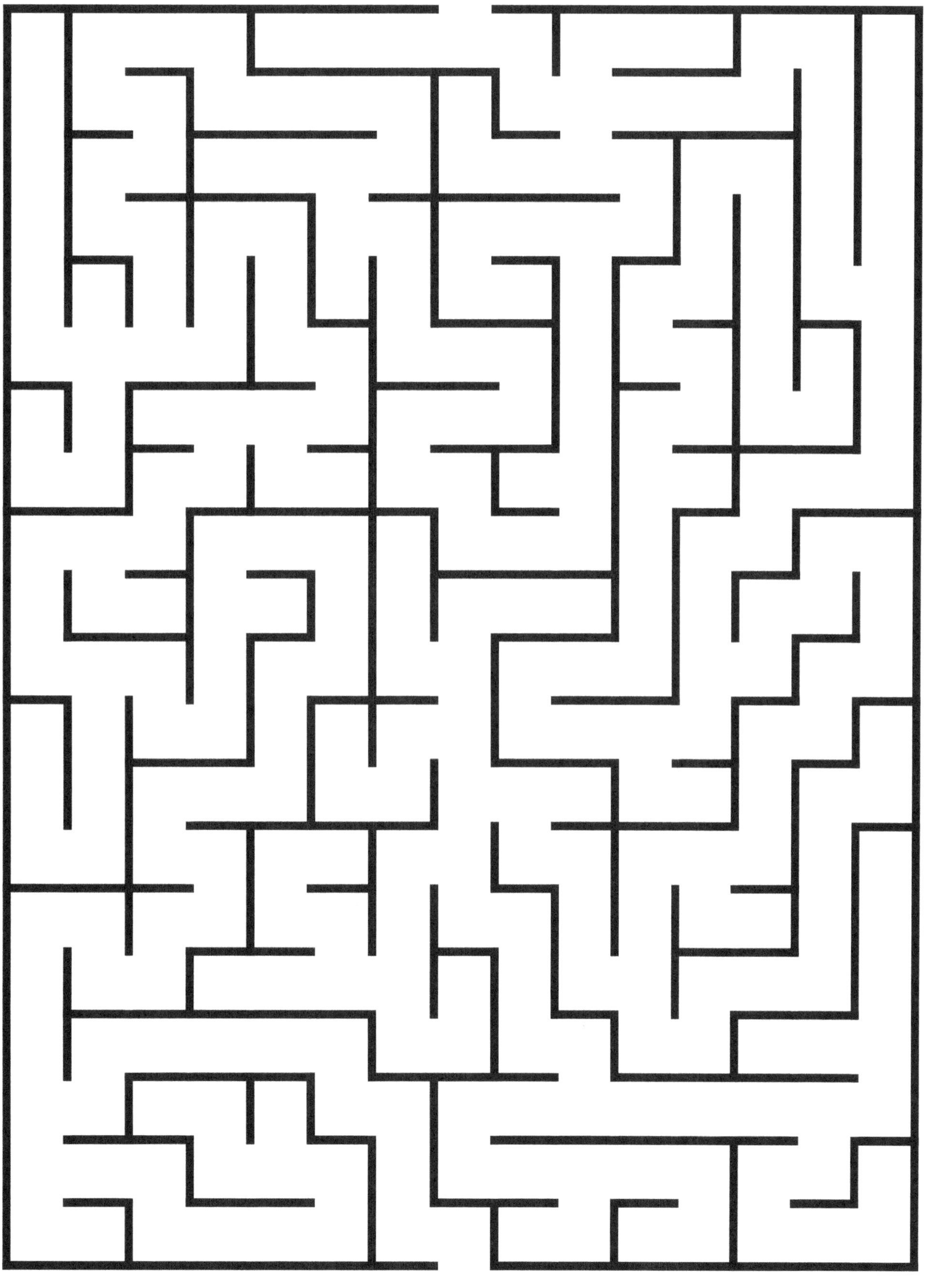

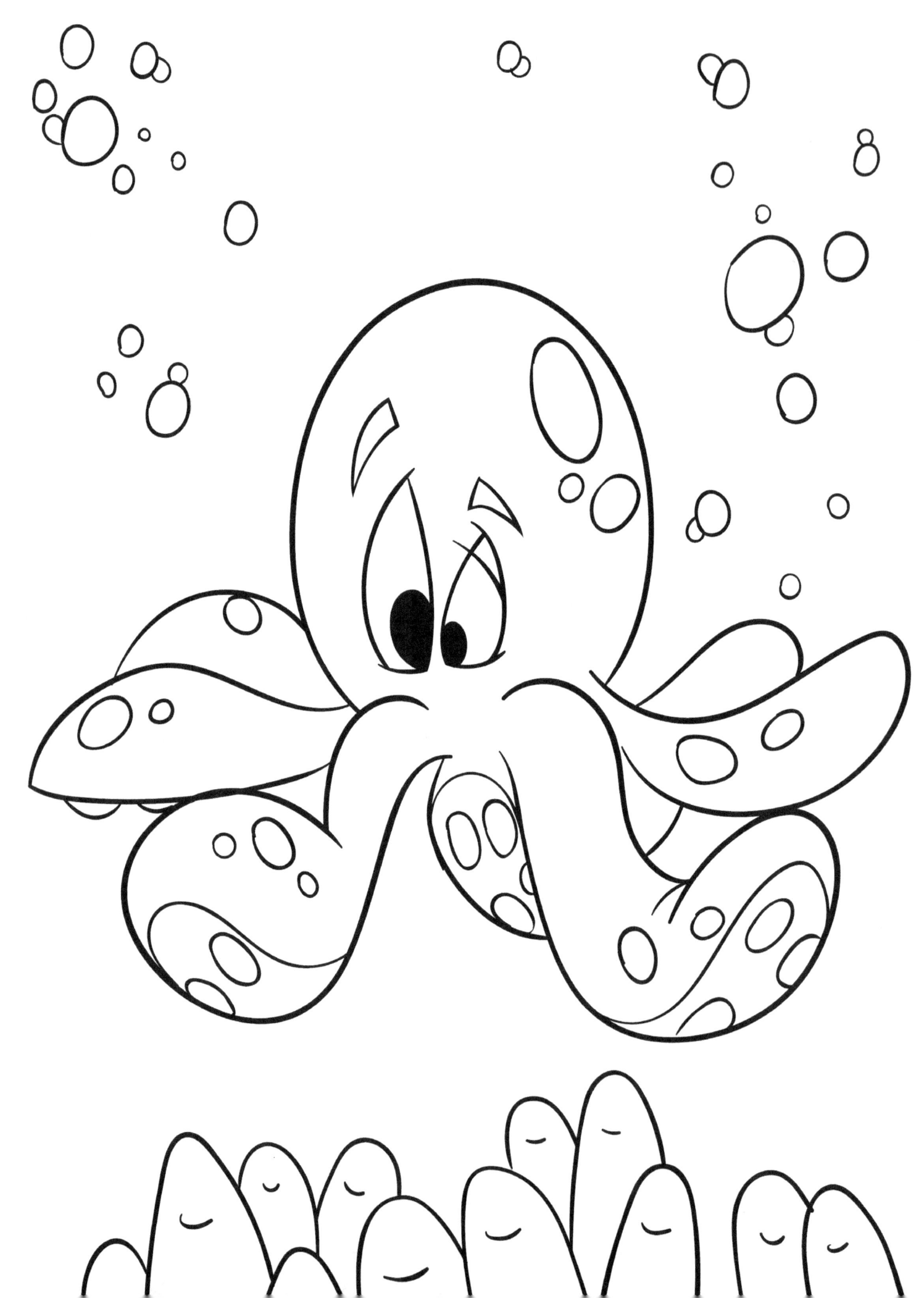

MATCH THE SHADOW

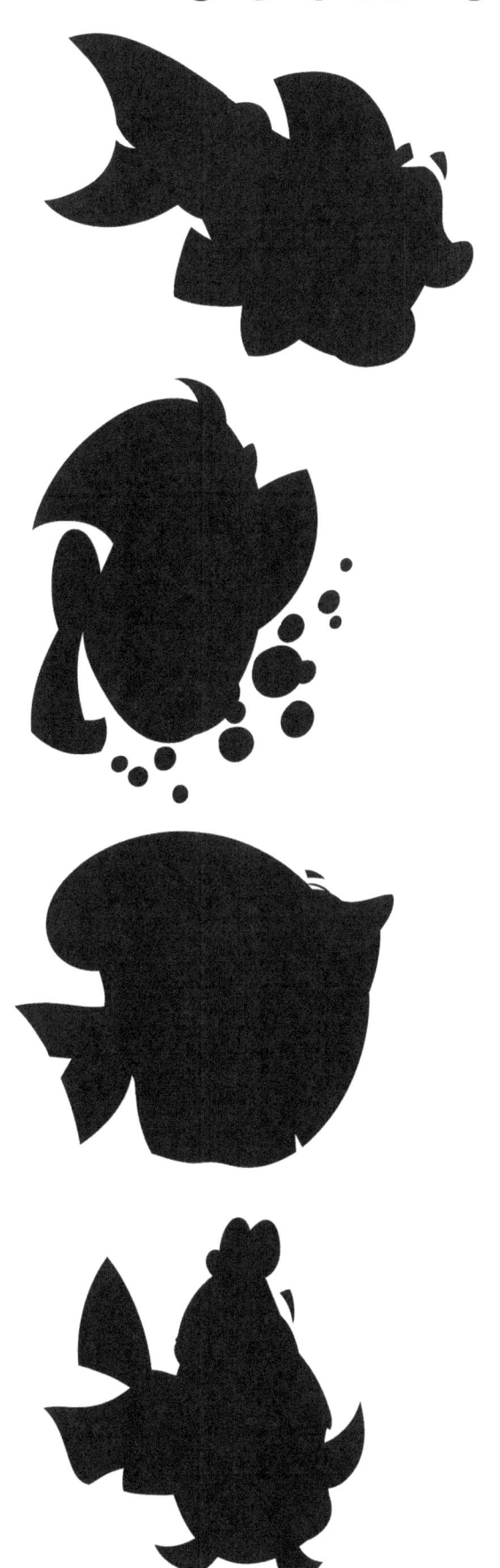
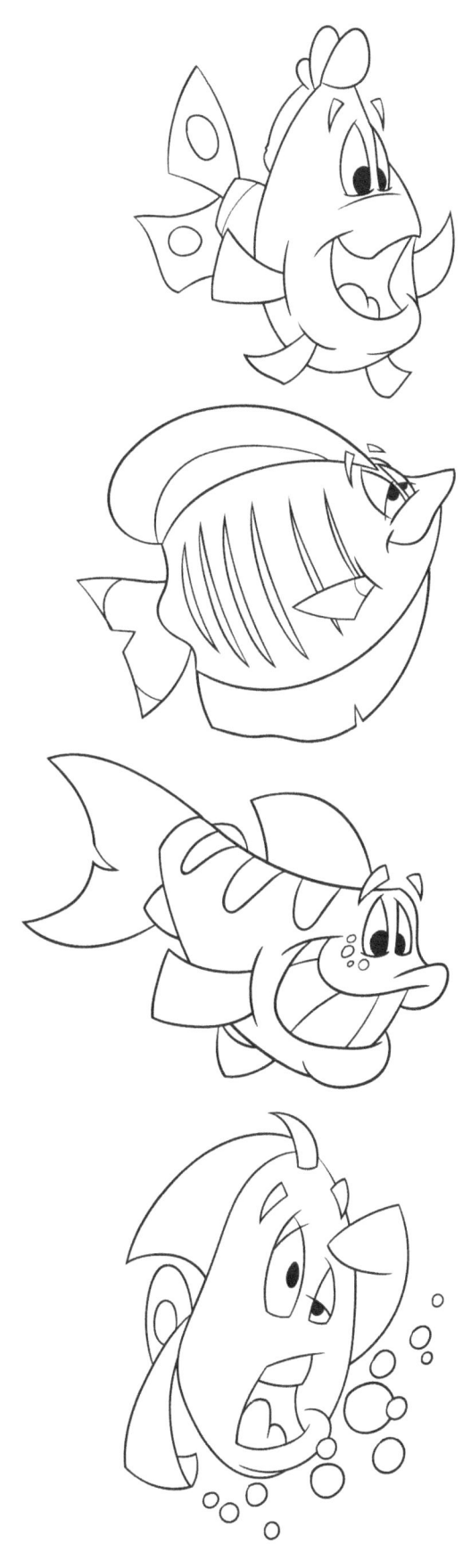

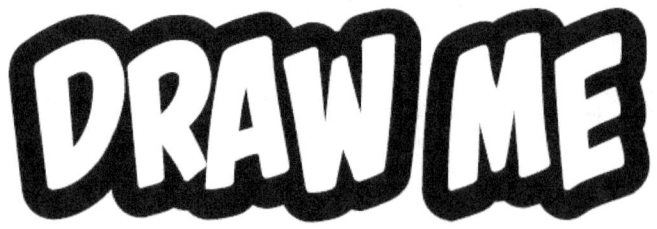

Use the grid to help you draw this fish.

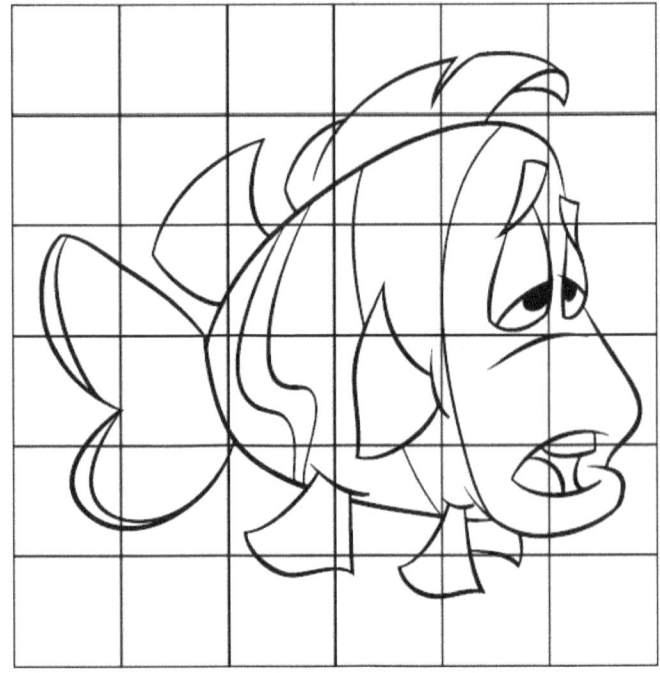

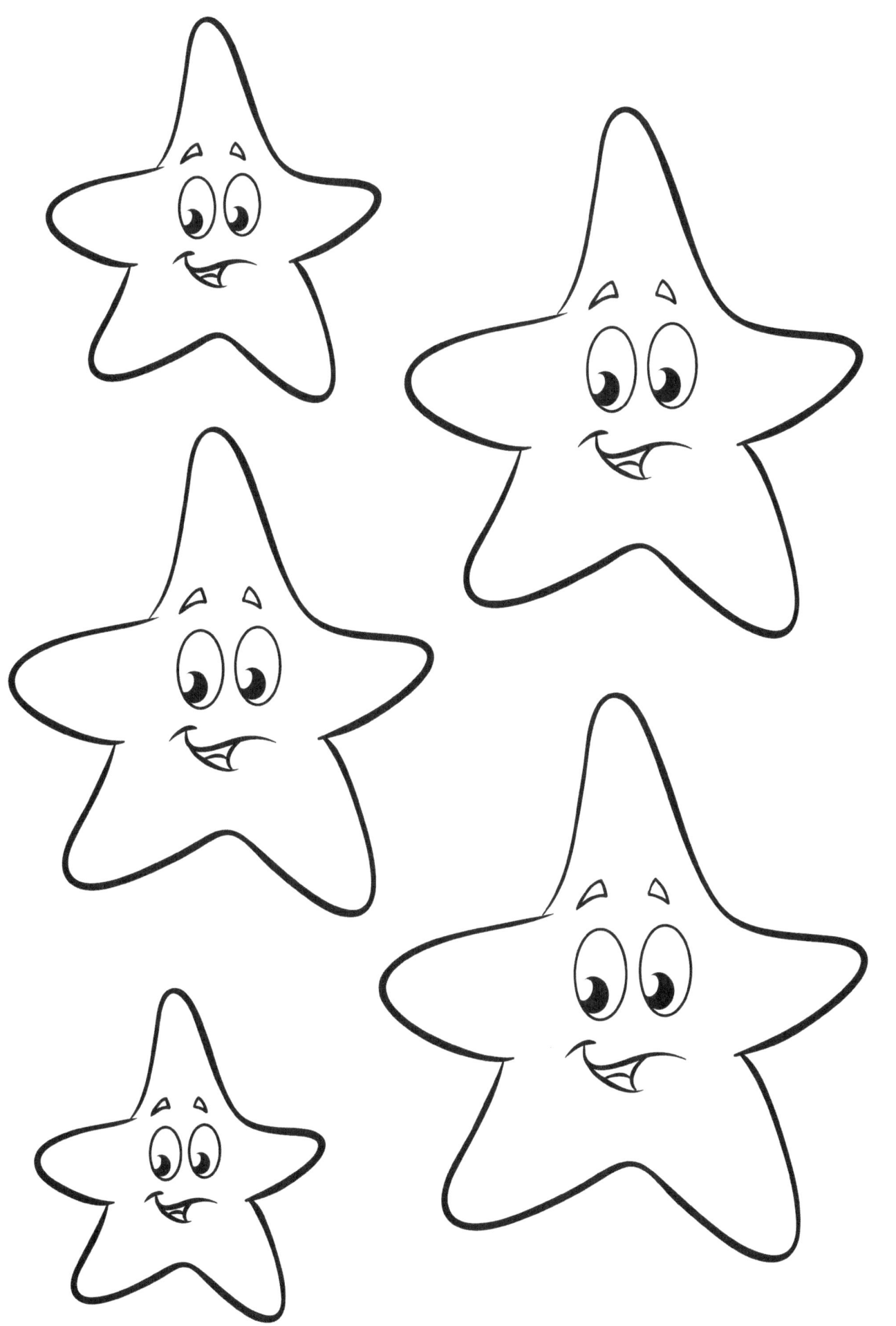

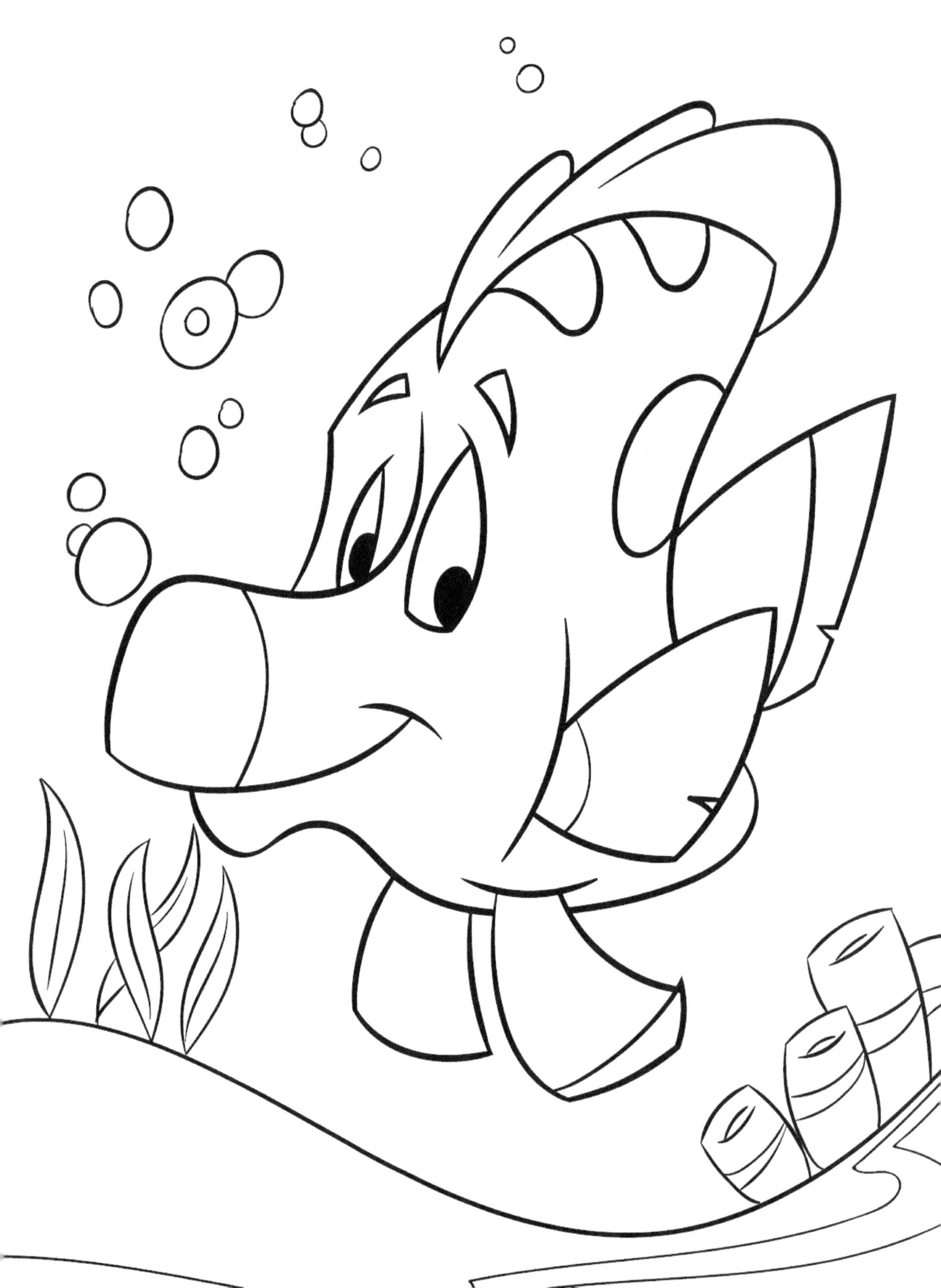

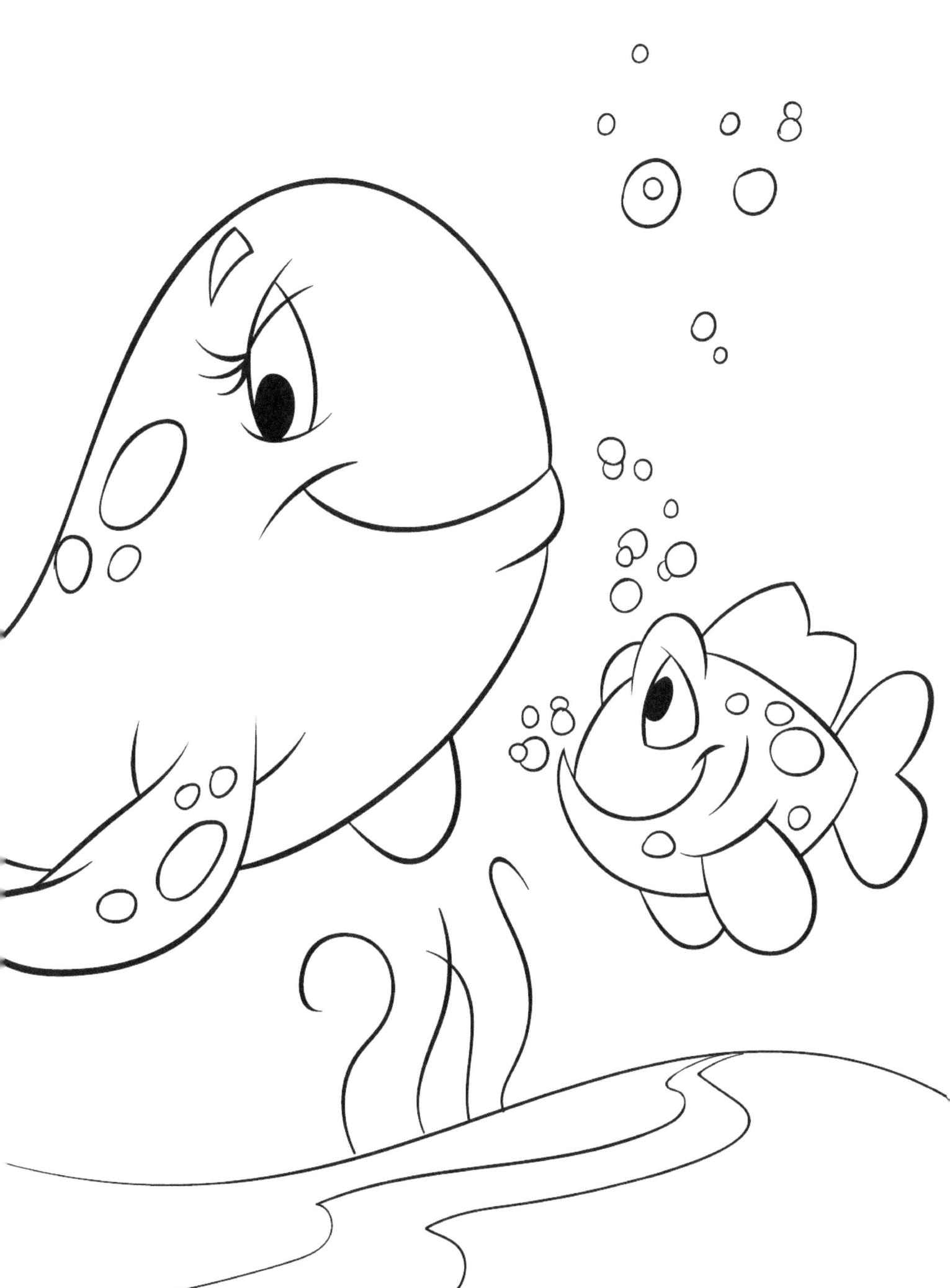

TIC-TAC-TOE

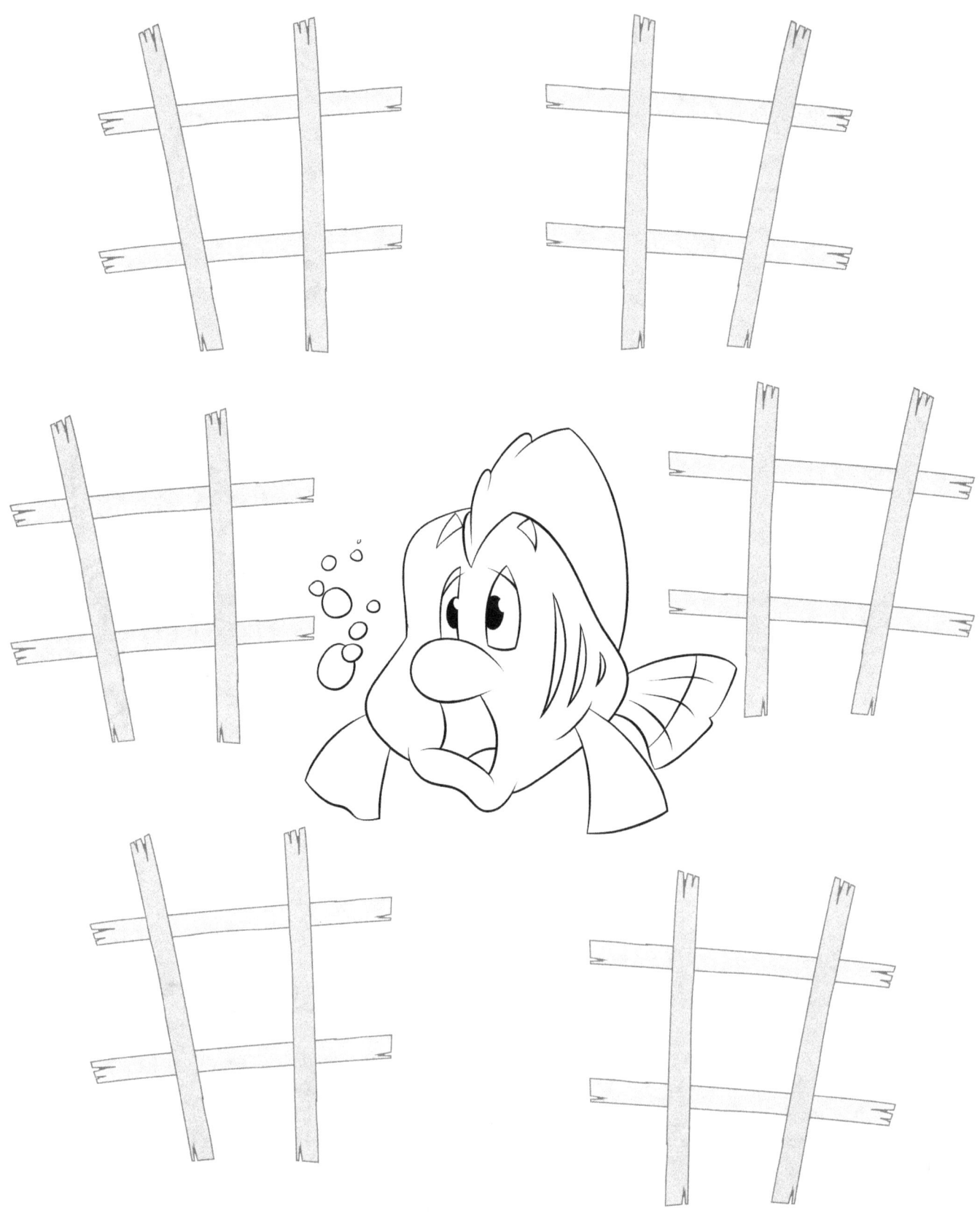

www.ingramcontent.com/pod-product-compliance
Lightning Source LLC
Chambersburg PA
CBHW062224220526
45471CB00009B/3334